Trading Places
Becoming My Mother's Mother

~ A Daughter's Memoir ~

Trading Places
Becoming My Mother's Mother

~ A Daughter's Memoir ~

SANDRA BULLOCK SMITH

Trading Places: Becoming My Mother's Mother
A Daughter's Memoir

ISBN: 978-0-9966924-1-0

Library of Congress Control Number: 2015914467

Cover design by Fiona Jayde, fionajaydemedia.com
Book design by Tamara Cribley, DeliberatePage.com
Edited by Mary Harris, www.maryharriswriter.com

This book is dedicated to my siblings and to our mother, Rebie Mooney Bullock. She taught us to love, laugh, share, eat our vegetables, and be kind to every living thing unless you were going to kill it for dinner. Her life was not easy, yet she was a living example of someone who did the best with what life handed her.

Thank you, Mom. We will always be grateful for the life lessons you taught and the love you shared.

My mother, Rebie Mooney Bullock.
March 19, 1922—January 13, 2015

"Most of all the beautiful things in life come by the twos and threes, by dozens and hundreds. Plenty of roses, stars, sunsets, rainbows, brothers and sisters, aunts and cousins, comrades and friends – but only one mother in the whole world."

~ Kate Douglas Wiggin

TRADING PLACES

I f your parent is fortunate enough to live to a ripe old age, there will come a point when you begin to notice a shift in power. The parent whose favorite words were "because I said so" is the one to whom you are tempted to say it right back. Role reversal is an emotional and intellectual challenge for parents. It is no less intense for an adult child. It is a labor of love to care for an elderly parent. AARP calls family caregivers "the backbone of the nation's long-term care system." I think we are more like the entire skeleton.

I started jotting down the things I said to Mom that were the same or similar to what she had said to me as a child. This mission of documenting these "mom-isms" started when Mom was in the hospital and needed a lot of care. That hospital stay was the catalyst for collecting these sayings, since I had many hours of sitting in a hospital room. Then the list sat in a computer file for years before I decided to share these stories.

As you read this book, you will no doubt recognize some of these phrases from your own childhood. I hope this brings you a smile. If you recognize some of these phrases from caring for an elderly parent, I hope it lightens your day and your burden. Caregiving is a labor, but it is definitely a labor of love.

"First we are children to our parents, then parents to our children, then parents to our parents, then children to our children."

~ Milton Greenblatt

INTRODUCTION

I spent ten years as a caregiver for my mother. It was not an easy job. Caring for any elderly person presents many challenges. Caring for an elderly parent is an emotional and physical test for which many children are not prepared. It is easy to fail this test. Even when by most people's standards you are passing the test, it can feel like failure.

I witnessed my mother change from an energetic and independent woman to an individual who was much like a child. During this transition, she was afflicted with many maladies: high blood pressure, diabetes, asthma, arthritis, congestive heart failure, and more. As she developed various medical conditions, we worked with her doctors and therapists to address them. For many years, I focused on getting her "better." I was an optimist, thinking we could fix whatever was wrong and that she would get better. My Baby Boomer generation is accustomed to walking into a physician's office and leaving with a diagnosis and a prescription to fix it. We want a name for what we have, and we want it to go away. It will be interesting to see how our generation ultimately deals with conditions that cannot be fixed. I am not looking forward to it.

For those in a caregiving role for a parent, there is a day when we realize our parent—that person who fixed things for us for years—is not going to get better. I remember being on the telephone with my friend Nancy when I had that realization. It had been a hard day for me. I told Nancy my mother didn't act like a mother any more. It was as if she was the child and I was the parent; we had traded places. This was the start of my journey through eldercare and the realization of how much it was like caring for a child. A child, however, is progressing, whereas the elderly ones are declining.

There is a delicate balance between dealing with a parent as if he or she is a child and treating the parent like a child. I tried to avoid the latter. I was not always successful. Nor was I always successful in not acting like a child myself.

As my mother moved into her eighties and nineties and her health declined, so did my hope for her conditions to improve. Somehow, by this point her decline was not so difficult to accept. Maybe by then I realized that dying was part of living. She had had a wonderful, full life. Now I just wanted her to have the best care for the final chapter. For me and my siblings, this meant trying to care for her in her home.

And so my journey through eldercare moved into a new territory— taking over or supervising most of her daily activities. She became legally blind during the time I cared for her, so even getting something to eat or drink became treacherous if she did it herself. Sometimes it was more dangerous for me than for Mom. She would spill things on the floor without knowing it, and I slipped and fell more than once as a result. I had to ban her from cooking. She would decide to cook something, often when I was out running errands. I would come home to find a pot smoking on the stove and Mom asleep in her chair.

It is easy to get frustrated, mad, and even depressed as a caregiver. The emotional and physical roller coasters are never-ending. Though you think you will get used to the ride, the highs and lows still surprise you after years of caring for a parent. I do not know if it's possible for an adult child to care for an elderly parent with a positive attitude all of the time. Perhaps there is a legion of perfect children out there who could pull this off, but I doubt it. My sister and I, who shared the majority of caregiving duties, would not be included in that number. We each went through a bevy of emotions, many of them the types of feelings we would teach our children to control—anger, despair, sadness, contempt, resentment, and anxiety. Then there was the guilt for having those emotions. Guilt is a despicable companion. Guilt knows where all your vulnerable spots are, and it does not bother to give you any warning of its visits.

Neither my sister Sarah nor I were working at the time when our mother began needing someone to care for her on a full-time basis. This was supposed to make it easier for us to care for her. However, we had other obstacles. For me, it was a geographic challenge. I lived 1400 miles away. I also have a very active lifestyle and travel a lot. To care for my mom, I would pack up my two dogs and my life and travel 1400 miles from Santa Fe, New Mexico to Shalimar, Florida. There were silver linings, though. I am now very proficient at packing a car. I listened to many audio books as I drove. My good friends in New Mexico, Charles and Nancy U., took care of my house and yard while I was gone. And I met some wonderful folks at a bed-and-breakfast in Bowie, Texas who let my dogs sleep with me when I stayed there. Martha and Bobby F. welcomed me and the pups like family every time I made that long drive. Their daughter Tracy and grandson Robby made a point to visit whenever I arrived. Robby liked to help me walk my dogs and talk classic rock. They all shared my grief when my dog Jake died. It was relationships like this that made the caregiving routine so much easier.

My sister Sarah also lived out of town and commuted 160 miles weekly to care for Mom. However, Sarah's biggest challenge was her own personal health issues. She was unable to work full-time due to a stroke she suffered at age fifty-one. I don't know why we didn't categorize caring for Mom as a full-time job. It was 24-7. If Mom didn't sleep, we didn't sleep. If Mom was hospitalized, we stayed at the hospital with her. Sarah struggled to manage the emotions of caring for Mom. I struggled with giving up so much of my life and the things I wanted to do. Then we both felt guilty for struggling with any of it. Guilt is a despicable companion.

Sarah and I split caring for Mom into seven-month and five-month duty periods. I cared for Mom for five months, seven days a week, twenty-four hours per day. Sarah cared for her for seven months, Sunday night through Friday afternoon, and my youngest brother Lloyd cared for mom over the weekends.

Lloyd lived eighty miles away, worked full-time, and gave up his weekends to care for Mom. He is an avid angler who frequently participates in weekend fishing tournaments. My mother realized what a jewel of a son she had when he joined the ranks of her caregivers. He was indispensable as part of Mom's caregiver team. He is also a great handyman and a pretty darn good cook. And you should have seen him putting curlers in Mom's hair with his giant hands. He could get all the curlers in Mom's hair, but I don't think he has a future in cosmetology. I think he would agree for many reasons.

As I said, I am an optimist. I try to find a silver lining in any given situation. Caring for an elderly parent doesn't give you many silver linings. But they are there. You would be astonished at the silver linings to which you wouldn't have given a second thought in your days prior to being a caregiver. You learn to celebrate and enjoy the small things, very much like you would when caring for a child: eating everything on her plate, pooping in the toilet, sleeping all night long, tying her own shoes, and unbridled laughter when I put her shoes on the wrong feet.

So there I was, trying to find as many bright spots in the situation as possible. Trying to be patient and loving. Trying to do what was right even though there were many times when there was no clearly "right" answer. And then my mom said "huh?" one time too many and I lost my cool. So why did that send me into a tizzy?

Mom didn't like to wear her (very expensive) hearing aids, so almost anything I said was responded to with "huh?" In response to her "huh?" one day, I told mom that "huh" was not a word and that as children we were not allowed to say "huh?" She huffed in exasperation and told me I was too fussy. At least she didn't say "huh?"

I began to realize how many times I said things to Mom that she had said to us as children. Talk about déjà vu. Of course, the tone I used when I said these things was different from the one she used with her kids. I firmly believed in not talking to her as if she were a child. That could be a challenge. However, just like the humor you experience while raising kids, there is some humor in eldercare. It's pretty funny when I think of all the things my mom said to me as a kid that I was now saying to her.

I remember the first time I had to ask Mom if she had wiped her rear end adequately. She had been very sick and her feeble state was affecting her ability to do even the simplest of self-care tasks. I wanted to cry. I probably did cry. However, I learned that it's better to remember when she asked me the same thing and smile about it. A wistful smile is better than a woeful grimace. Wondering about her butt-wiping abilities was a big dose of woeful. Sometimes you can overcome woe with a wistful smile. Sometimes woe wins.

So I started writing down things Mom said to me as a child that I was now saying to her. I realized how much of my time was spent mothering my mother. I started looking for reading material that would help me cope with the challenges of trading places. I was fortunate to find and read the book Mothering Mother: A Daughter's Humorous and Heartbreaking Memoir by Carol O'Dell. It was a used copy that had been autographed at some point in its life. Ms. O'Dell had written under her signature, "Tell your stories." That inspired me to attempt to turn my list into a book that could be enjoyed by others. It also made me realize that things could be a lot worse. Ms. O'Dell had to deal with many more challenges due to her mother's affliction with Alzheimer's disease. I was very thankful for having a sweet, gracious mother who still had a good grasp on the real world most of the time.

For all you wonderful children who provide loving care to a parent, I hope this book gives you a laugh, a smile and a little inspiration. You already have had enough tears. Just remember, sometimes you have to laugh to keep from crying.

"If you want to touch the past, touch a rock. If you want to touch the present, touch a flower. If you want to touch the future, touch a life."

~ Author Unknown

My mother as a beautiful young woman. My father wrote in a card to her,
"You remind me of flowers. Natural beauty and love combined." We should
always remember to see elderly people as a culmination of an amazing life.

CHAPTER 1

Life Lessons

am one of five siblings. We were raised in a loving, happy home. Our mother was a first-grade teacher and our father was a master sergeant in the Air Force. My parents had a very modest income and lifestyle. These days we would call it poor. Hand-me-downs were a fact of life, as were shared bedrooms, shared chores, and shared family meals.

While I wish we had been better off financially, I realize now that my parents and my modest upbringing taught me many valuable life lessons. When I was in a parenting role for my mother, these lessons helped me deal with being a caregiver.

Honesty really is the best policy.

Sometimes the message isn't easy, and sometimes the truth causes more angst. In the end, finding a way to be gently honest means you are still treating your parent like an adult, even though you are managing him or her as a child. This doesn't apply to being brutally honest, though. Sometimes the truth was sugarcoated for us as children.

"Honey, just because you are missing your two front teeth doesn't make you look ugly. Just ignore those kids who call you snaggle-puss!"

Sugarcoating the truth for a parent can be a great strategy.

You can't sugarcoat the reality of caregiving, though. It's a tough job. But you can avoid making your parent feel like they are a burden by sugarcoating your reality.

Grief is part of life.

As an adult, I did not have a dog for years, even though I really wanted one. A colleague asked me why I didn't get a dog and my response was, "I don't want to go through losing it." He suggested to me that I was losing a lot of joy by not having a dog, just to avoid the grief of enduring its death. He was right. I needed to accept that grief and dying would happen. What we do with the rest of our time on this planet makes those natural elements of life easier to endure. I am on my third dog since receiving that advice. Losing my first dog hurt just as badly as I thought it would, but the love I received really did make the pain worth it.

I knew that I would lose my mother someday. On days when caring for her was particularly challenging, I imagined how sad it would be without her. It helped me keep my attitude straight.

Crying is good for the soul.

I am not an advocate of pity parties. They allow you to wallow in misery and drag yourself even further into the depths of woe. But sometimes having a good cry is like changing the oil in your car. You got 3000 miles out of that batch, now you have 3000 miles to go before another. Clean out the pipes and get ready for a new run. I like to cry in the bathtub. That way, no one notices your red face and you don't ruin your makeup. Also, if you wait until bath time to cry, often you get over the need for it before then.

Laughing is better.

Sometimes you have to laugh to keep from crying. No matter the reason, a good laugh is good medicine. Laughing at yourself is like an antibiotic—it gets rid of a lot of harmful stuff. And there are no bad side effects. No one ever got a yeast infection from laughing.

Everyone needs a hero.

My circle of friends contains many heroes who helped me get through rough times. Nancy U., Connie P., Dawn C., Sue Z., Sabrina H., Michele C., and Maria F. all came to my rescue at some point. My heroes helped me by reminding me how strong I was, by listening to me, and by telling me that everything would work out. They found humor in my stories and shared their stories, which took my mind off me. Your heroes are at your fingertips. Reach out and touch them, even when you don't think you need to.

Forgive and forget.

You only get so much emotional energy each day. Harboring ill feelings drains your emotional battery quickly. As a caregiver, you will be mad at your parent at some point. If you are having a hard time letting go of the anger, use the 15-minute rule. Stay mad for 15 minutes, have your hissy fit in private, and then get over it. Really get over it—that's the "forget" part of this. Forgive the situation and put it behind you. Your heart will feel lighter if you forgive and forget.

Apologies make you a bigger person.

I have apologized many times when I technically didn't have to. Apologizing doesn't always mean you are wrong and the other person is right. It means you value your relationship more than your ego. Taking the high road in any situation is a class act. There is something cathartic about a genuine apology. Not like when we were kids and Mom forced us into an apology.

"Sandra, you apologize for putting a lizard in your sister's bed! Then you both hug each other."

"I am sorry you are such a sissy that a little lizard would scare you."

"Young lady, that is not an apology. You apologize like you mean it."

"Well, she's lucky I didn't catch a big lizard that would have really clamped on to her. Oh, all right. I'm soooooooorry. But she has to hug me first."

Of course, the real lesson in apologizing is to learn to avoid doing and saying things that might require an apology. Imagine that an apology is like a nail in a wall. You can apologize and take the nail out of the wall, but there is still a hole there. There is extra work to actually repair the hole. Better to have not put a hole in the wall in the first place.

No one gets it right all of the time.

There is a lot of power in the statement, "I was wrong." I remember working with a woman who thought she was never wrong. Even when she was wrong, she was quick to point out that if she was wrong, it was someone else's fault. The frustration of dealing with her taught me the value of owning my mistakes. Owning a mistake provides you the opportunity to learn from it. I like being right. It feels good to be right. It also feels good to say, "I was wrong."

Sometimes there is no right answer.

Oh, for a crystal ball to help find the right answer. There were so many times while caring for Mom when there was no clearly right answer. In fact, there have been so many times in my life when there was no clearly right answer. When I worked in Human Resources at Blue Cross and Blue Shield of Louisiana, my staff would come to me for answers about various issues. My typical response was a question (or many questions). I could easily tell them what to do but I wanted them to learn to develop their own decision-making abilities.

I remember Karen D. celebrating the first time she came in with all the questions answered ahead of time. The point of my questions was to get them to think things through. When making decisions, whether for your parent or for yourself, the best approach is to think through the options carefully, then go with the one that makes the most sense. Sounds easy, huh? On days when there is no best option, when all the options have repercussions that cause their own problems, decision-making is just another cause for angst. Not making a decision usually is worse. So take your best shot and learn from there.

There is always someone who has it worse than you.

This reminds me of my mom telling us about the starving children in India as she was requiring us to eat Brussels sprouts. What kid enjoys that? There were times when I wished I didn't have to take care of my mother. I wanted my life back. Then I thought of the people out there who had lost a parent, and I knew some of them would have gladly traded places. I also know people who have grouchy, ill-tempered, ungrateful elderly parents. I was blessed to have a mom who was gracious, sweet and thankful to have her family helping her. I was blessed to have a mom to care for. And thanks to my friends Don and Dawna G. and their excellent culinary skills, I learned to enjoy Brussels sprouts too.

If you have nothing nice to say, don't say anything at all.

A few years ago, my brother Lloyd taught me to say, "That sounds like a great idea." Even when it didn't. I am often critical and demanding. I know that about myself. When something was done for me and it wasn't quite right, I said so. I thought I was being honest. My brother made me realize that being brutally honest is not always the best policy. I've learned to say, "How nice," and "That's a great idea" when I really wanted to say, "What the heck were you thinking?" There is a lot to be said for keeping your mouth shut and your ears open. Mom always said you can't hear with your mouth open.

You always have a choice to be positive or negative.

Choose to be positive. Negative will come to you often enough without making an active choice to go there. Even when you believe in silver linings, some days it is hard to find one. When I was struggling with decisions about moving Mom into an assisted-living facility, I felt like everything in my life was out of order. I like having my ducks in a row and my ducks were scattered all over the place with no immediate chance to get them marching along in an orderly fashion. My friend Nancy, who knows how anal I am about order, had some helpful positive words for me when I was telling her about my situation. "Well" she said, "at least you have ducks."

Say or do something nice every day.

When you do nice things, you feel nice. My friend George G. once told me that I was far too accustomed to having my way, and that I should do something I didn't want to do every day. I thought that was good advice. I started by letting bad drivers who didn't know how to merge onto an interstate pull in front of me without blowing my horn. Then I realized letting people do stupid things on the road and not reacting in an ugly manner felt good. I stopped honking the horn and cutting people off. It felt nice. I became a kinder, gentler driver. That one change helped me smooth some of the sharp edges in other areas of my life.

I think one of the best surprises is when someone does something nice for you for no reason at all. When Mom was in the nursing home for rehabilitation after hospital stays, she had roommates whom I continued to visit after mom was discharged. These elderly ladies seemed genuinely touched that someone would go out of their way to bring them something to read and a sweet treat. They were always happy to have a visitor. It was a nice thing to do and I always felt happier because of it.

Believe your day will be good.

My mother was a happy woman. She always believed in the good in people and in life. She taught us to do the same. As an adult, another perspective on optimism was shared when I met a young Navajo woman in Monument Valley. She told me she started each day giving thanks for the day. She said every morning, before anything happens, you have the opportunity to be thankful for what may come during the day, and believe it will be good. She said the end of her daily prayers was a phrase she repeated four times, "It will be beautiful." What a great way to start your day—believing good things will happen and that your day will be beautiful.

Keep your word.

Your character is defined by doing what you say you will do. You should be known for being dependable. If you say you are going to do something, then do it. If you can't commit to doing something, then say you can't. There is a lot wrong with saying "yes" and meaning "no."

Do unto others.

Mom taught us "The Golden Rule" and reminded us of it throughout our lives. It is such a simple yet profound way to measure your own actions, and it can apply to every aspect of your life. Mom considered the "do" part of that statement to include thoughts as well. I think it was one reason she was so well-balanced and positive. It's a great guide to consider when caring for someone else.

I hope if I am fortunate enough to grow old, there will be someone who will care for me as I cared for my mother. Since I don't have children, I don't know who that will be.

When my nieces Katrina and Jessica were little girls, they asked me who would get my jewelry when I died. I told them that old women need to go to Walmart and to doctors' appointments. Therefore, when I became an old woman, whoever took me to Walmart and to my doctors' appointments would get my stuff. I told them they might want to consider being that person. Katrina said, "But we will have to take care of our mom when she is old." I told her that I had better jewelry than her mom so she might want to be prepared to take care of both of us.

The reality for me is that my caregiver is likely to be totally unrelated to me. I hope he or she knows and lives by The Golden Rule. I also hope he or she reads this book and has a good sense of humor.

"Love is an action verb."

~ Author Unknown

CHAPTER 2

"Don't say 'huh'."

"Huh is not a word!"

I don't know how many times I heard that as a child. Using "huh," "ain't," and "yeah" were not tolerated well by my schoolteacher mother. That grammar lesson stuck with me all these years. My family is never surprised when I correct their grammar. Mom didn't raise us to talk like rednecks.

As an adult I say, "Pardon me?" or "Excuse me?" Or in the case of my husband, whose voice level is just a hair above a whisper, I say, "When I ask you to repeat yourself it's because you are speaking too softly. There is nothing wrong with my hearing." I think he would disagree with me.

My husband tells me that I will be deaf when I get old since I like to listen to loud music. I tell him that it will probably be a blessing. I won't be able to hear him complain. My husband is an endurance runner who routinely punishes his joints with insanely long runs. He won't be able to walk and I won't be able to hear him complain about it.

I thought my grammatically correct upbringing was why hearing my mother say "Huh?" irritated me so much. Now I see that was a convenient excuse. When I pondered it, I realized I was bothered by this example of my mother's decline.

Mom had been deaf in one ear since childhood as a result of the mumps. The ear she could hear out of—her "good" ear—was bad on a good day. The best way to talk to her was to get her attention and then say what you had to say. It took me a while to figure that out. I would start to ask her a question. "Mom, what do you…?"

"Huh?"

"I said, what do you…?"

"Huh?"

And so it went. One day I was so undone by all the "huhs" that I went out in the back yard where she couldn't hear me and started yelling, "HUH?! HUH?! HUH?! HUH?!" The neighbors must've thought I was crazy. In a way, I was. But I got a lot of therapy by standing out in the yard yelling.

The next time she said, "Huh?" I said, "Huh is not a word. Don't you remember telling us that when we were kids?"

"Well, I didn't hear what you said." She totally missed the point. And I totally learned to get over it. That eased the frustration for both of us.

Now, every once in a while I say, "Huh?" just to see how it feels. I don't like it. It's just not right. I expect the person to whom I'm speaking to look at me with raised eyebrows and admonish me. In fact, my husband recently told me he didn't like hearing me say "Huh?" I know how he feels.

I feel like I'm getting away with something when my "Huh?" goes unnoticed.

I am pretty sure I will have hearing issues if I live to be an old woman. But you will not hear me saying "Huh?"

The start of a big family. Mom loved being a mother even though
she had her hands full. She told me since she got a late start on
childbearing, she didn't allow much time in between pregnancies. Her
first child, Sarah, was born in 1956 and her last (fifth) child, Lloyd,
was born in 1963. This photo was taken in 1960. Left to right is Mom,
Luther at age 1, Sandra at age 3 and Sarah at age 4.

CHAPTER 3

"Don't give your food to the dog."

As children, we were taught to eat what was placed in front of us. My mother cooked dinner for us every evening after working all day. She got creative with a tight food budget, and we were expected to clean our plates with no complaining. It wasn't always easy to pull that off, even though she was a very good cook.

One of our most unusual dinners was barbecued bologna. Mom really knew how to get a lot of mileage out of a little meat. She also had a garden. We always had veggies from the garden as well as low-priced frozen vegetables. Some were better than others. We children were thankful to have a dog who knew that the best place during mealtime was underneath the dining room table. The kids in our family developed real stealth when it came to slipping unwanted food down to the dog. At least, we thought we were being stealthy.

"Don't give your food to the dog!" meant we had been caught passing Brussels sprouts and other unwanted morsels to the canine vacuum cleaner. My parents caught on to our game and the dog was banished to the backyard during mealtimes. He couldn't wait to get back in after meals to scoop up the things we "accidentally" dropped. Dogs are smart that way.

My mother loved dogs. She had two spoiled Chihuahuas who lived in her lap. Tonka was a sweet little six-pounder. Taffy looked like a canine version of Jabba the Hutt, the really fat, slug-like character in Star Wars. She had Jabba's disposition as well. She weighed in at fourteen pounds until she lost a bit of weight because of diabetes. Mom's habit of feeding her dogs from her plate was a contributing factor to Taffy's rotund girth.

Yes, the same mother who chastised us for giving our food to the dog was constantly feeding the dogs from her own plate. To my mother, food was love. When she sat down with a plate of food, the dogs immediately went to her chair and sat at her feet. They knew she could not resist those sweet eyes looking up at her. And she thought that by sharing her meal with the dogs, she was sharing her love. It didn't matter what she was eating. "Look at how these dogs love green beans," she would say. "Look at the mess you made on the carpet," is what I wanted to say as she tossed green beans onto the floor for the poor, starving dogs.

Her dogs would perch on her lap and jump to catch the tidbits that Mom dropped from her plate. I finally convinced Mom that having the dogs on her lap while she ate was a bad idea. We had countless dog fights when Taffy and my dog Katie both dove for something she'd thrown on the floor. "Don't give your food to the dogs!" I cannot count the number of times I said this to my mom.

Mom would attempt to justify giving her food to the dogs. "Well, it was a tough piece that I couldn't chew," she would say. Or, "I can't finish eating all this food."

Taffy's diabetes was the only way I was able to get Mom to reduce the amount of people food she gave to the dogs. I gave up hoping that she would stop entirely. I explained how we needed to control what Taffy ate and when she ate. I added that rice pudding was not part of the plan, even if Taffy loved it. Her response? "Taffy, that mean lady over there won't let me give you any." I guess that sometimes you have to be the bad guy.

Some days, I thought I had really gotten through to her about feeding the dogs from her plate. But as I left the room to take my plate into the kitchen, I would glance back over my shoulder in time to see a quick flick of the wrist and a happy dog. I guess every dog has his day.

The dogs knew to get close to Mom when she was eating. In her eyes, food was love. Even with dogs. Tonka is on the left; Taffy and Lloyd's dogs Pixie and Lola are on the right. Mom loved dogs almost as much as she loved children.

CHAPTER 4

"Can't never could."

My mother was the type of mom who encouraged her kids to learn. Whether we were learning to tie our shoelaces, learning algebra, learning to cook, sew or parallel park, Mom was there to encourage us. When we said, "I can't," her response was, "Can't never could."

In kindergarten, I was sick when my classmates learned to tie their shoelaces. Back then, shoes only came with laces. Velcro would have been really handy the week we had our shoe-tying test in kindergarten. Faced with the possibility of failing the test, I invented my own shoe-tying technique. I passed the test and continued to tie my shoes in my own fashion until I was an adult. My dad got a real kick out of watching me tie my shoes. I eventually learned the proper shoe-tying technique. I never forgot how important it is to try rather than simply accept failure.

Often when a child says, "I can't," a parent is tempted to do it for them. I was lucky to be raised by a mom who made us learn, partially because there were so many of us that she couldn't do it all if she wanted to. But fortunately for us, she saw the value in having us do for ourselves. We were blessed to be taught so many things in a loving, patient manner.

My mother's vision, mobility, and cognition all declined in the last years before her passing. She was legally blind, wore a brace on her leg, and often couldn't remember that she had eaten just thirty minutes ago. Dressing could be exhausting for her. She had to wear special shoes to fit over her brace. Nothing fit her easily.

When she lived at home, she still wanted to help in the house. She had a difficult time grasping and holding things, or even seeing what she was trying to help with. When she told me something like, "I can't mix this together," or, "I can't reach the salt," I would tell her, "Can't never could."

That sounds mean, right? My point in saying that to her was that I didn't know if she needed help with the task at hand, or if she needed me to do it because she really couldn't. I am a problem solver. I liked to find ways to enable her to do the things she tried to do. I asked her not to tell me that she couldn't do something, but to tell me what she needed.

"I can't find the cheese in the refrigerator" turned into "Would you get the cheese for me?" "I can't turn my lamp on" turned into "Would you find a lamp that I can manage?" Sometimes she really couldn't do the task. Sometimes she needed me to find a modification so that she could. Sometimes it was really simple; sometimes it wasn't. Sometimes I couldn't fix everything, but I never forgot to try.

CHAPTER 5

"Are you going to sleep all day?"

The sleep habits of children are probably one of the most frustrating subjects for many parents. It sure was at our house. During the school year, we all got up and ate breakfast together at the family table. We lived for Saturday when we were allowed to sleep in. The older we got, the more we wanted to sleep in. And if it was cold outside, forget it. We did not want to get out of bed. But there were things that needed to be done—everything from haircuts to chores. "Are you going to sleep all day?" was tossed into bedrooms, usually starting around 8:00 a.m. on Saturdays. It wasn't long after that when we were ordered out of bed. I have no idea what time my mom got up back in those days. Early. Way too early.

Elderly people sleep a lot. I mean a lot. It's hard to manage an elderly person's sleep. With my mom, some nights she slept so poorly that she really needed to nap during the day. But on the other hand, if she slept all day, there was a good chance that she would have another sleepless night. It was a real Catch-22.

When I first started caring for Mom, she would sleep all afternoon. This was after a lengthy nap in the morning. Back then, she was still able to dress herself so she slept in every morning until she was ready to get up and get dressed. I would usually hear her moving around by 8:00 a.m. On mornings when she still hadn't stirred by 9:00 a.m., I would start worrying about her. I always feared going into her bedroom and finding that she had passed away during the night. I would quietly slip into her room and watch her to see if she was breathing. If she seemed to be okay, I would slip back out and let her sleep if she had had a rough night.

My deadline for Mom getting up was 9:30 a.m. If she slept beyond that, I knew her day would be all messed up. Sometimes I called my sister Sarah and asked her to call the house so the phone would wake Mom up. It let me avoid being the whip-cracker who was getting her out of bed earlier than what she probably deemed necessary.

But usually, I was the one at her door letting her know it was time to get up.

I'd ask her, "Are you going to sleep all day?" I'd say it in a lighthearted manner. No matter what, Mom still deserved to be talked to in a polite, respectful manner.

"Isn't it early yet?" she would respond. Maybe it was early. Too early. It's all relative.

Mom was a multitasker before the phrase was invented.
She could do many things with a baby tucked under her arm
and children all around her. Circa 1963.

CHAPTER 6

"Turn that down!"

I guess anyone who has endured the teenage years of a child has yelled this phrase on more than one occasion. I have always been afflicted with the need to play my music loudly. My older sister was worse than I was. I think she has gotten over her loud music days unless Bruce Springsteen is playing. Me, well, I still love to turn up the volume.

As a teenager, one of my favorite albums was Joe Cocker's "Mad Dogs and Englishmen." I would rattle the windows playing that album. My sister Sarah went through this Patti Smith phase. We had dueling stereos. That is, until we heard "Turn that down!" yelled down the hall. I'm surprised we could hear it. We always complied, but every few minutes we would slip the volume up a notch. It was a battle of the wills. How often did my mom want to come back to our bedrooms and yell over the music, only to be aggravated by it again a little while later? We figured we could win that battle. She had more stuff to do than we did. But Mom always won in the end. "If you girls have to be told one more time to turn that noise down, I will take those stereos away from you!"

Mom never threatened to do things that she did not intend to follow through on. We didn't have any of that "I'm going to count to three" stuff. We knew by the tone of her voice that she meant what she said.

As I mentioned earlier, my mother had profound hearing loss. She was totally deaf in one ear and not much better in the other ear. When her hearing loss became a barrier to conversations and church sermons, she invested in a high-tech digital hearing aid. She hated it. For a while, she would wear it to church, but later she quit even that. She said the hearing aid made her sound like a squeaky old woman when she was singing. Truth is, even before she started wearing a hearing aid she sounded like a squeaky old woman when she sang. I am sure God appreciated her efforts, though.

During the day, Mom liked to watch TV. Her choice of TV shows killed me. Not literally, of course, but some days it was hard to believe my college-educated, smart mother spent time watching judge shows. She watched Judge Alex, Judge Joe Brown, and her favorite, Judge Judy. The content of these shows was enough to make me leave the room. Couple that with room-rattling volume and it was enough to make you wish the power would go out.

"Mom, we have to turn the volume down."

"Huh?"

I wanted to scream. I was bombarded by noise when I was at Mom's house. My house is out in the country. You can hear a bird fly over. I love the peace of sitting with no TV or any other man-made noise to ruin the ambience.

My mother's house was two houses away from a six-lane highway and directly across from the town hall and police station. So even if Mom didn't have the television on at a ridiculously loud level, there was enough noise to make you wish your hearing was temporarily impaired. Then you add a blaring television with some woman's "baby daddy" arguing about why he shouldn't have to pay child support since he may not be the baby daddy…well, it was just too much for me.

I begged Mom to wear her hearing aid. For a woman who never made excuses about anything, she became adept at making excuses for not wearing her hearing aid. To solve the problem of the too-loud TV, my brother Lloyd found a personal amplifier that worked pretty well. We positioned the receiver so it would pick up our conversations as well as the TV. We went through a lot of batteries but it was worth it to have the TV judges not rattling the windows.

Mom also liked to listen to church singing when she went to bed for the evening. We bought a portable CD player for her and adapted the buttons so she could operate it. Since she went to bed much earlier than I did, the volume of the church hymns didn't matter much. She would be in her room with the door closed while I watched television. But sometimes she would wake up in the middle of the night and decide to listen to music if she couldn't get back to sleep. That was a problem. We all love to hear "Amazing Grace," but 2:00 a.m. is not my favorite time to hear it.

I bought Mom some headphones and that solved the problem. She could play her church music at any time of the night and it didn't disturb me.

One night, I awoke with a jolt. The noise coming from Mom's room was otherworldly. I jumped out of bed and ran toward my mom's room, expecting to find her writhing in pain. As I approached the door, I realized it was just one of the CDs from a church singing program. Whoever was closest to the microphone needed a singing lesson or two. Mom was singing along, sounding a lot like a squeaky old lady.

The headphone jack had come out of the player and Mom hadn't figured that out.

"Mom! Turn that down!"

"Huh?"

"Your music, it's too loud. Turn it down or put your headphones on!"

"I thought I had my headphones on."

And she did. They just weren't plugged into the CD player. We got her hooked back up properly and I got her a glass of milk. I went back to bed hoping that she would fall asleep before she managed to disconnect the earphones again.

Mom loved to read. When her eyesight started to fail, we switched to large-print books. When she could no longer read large-print books, we bought her audio books and used the "Talking Books for the Blind." This is a free service for those with severe visual impairment.

CHAPTER 7

"Did you want your hair that color?"

My mother never asked me about my hair color. I had no need to add more color to my hair—it was flaming red when I was a kid. Growing up with freckles and red hair was bad enough without adding a purple stripe or two to my hair.

These days, though, the kids with neon hair definitely outnumber the redheads. We redheads just thought we had colorful tresses. I can imagine the reaction of parents when a child turns up with a head full of purple hair, or even just a few neon streaks. Add that to some of the spikes and Mohawks and you have some seriously individualized hairstyles. I don't think parents get it. It's all about being an individual. Some kids express their individuality in less stressful ways than others. If my mom had asked me if I wanted red hair, I would have said, "No."

She once told my Aunt Edna that all of her girls colored their hair. "Mom," I said, "I have never colored my hair."

"Well, yes you have. It's a totally different color than when you were younger."

"You are right about that, Mom, but the color has changed with age, not with chemicals."

She looked at me like I was trying to pull the wool over her eyes. "Honest, Mom. I have never colored my hair. If I am going to tell you a lie, it won't be about my hair color."

My mom had beautiful silver hair. She never had her hair colored. That's one thing she and I had in common. Mom had a great method to keep any yellow from sneaking into her silvery mane—she put just a drop or two of Mrs. Stewart's Bluing solution in her conditioning rinse. I don't think many women from my generation know about Mrs. Stewart's. It's a blue dye that you add in very small quantities to the whites in your laundry to keep them from yellowing. It works great with silver hair too. Unless you add too much.

For her hair rinse, Mom would mix up a small pitcher of warm water with a drop or two of Mrs. Stewart's and a bit of conditioner. A drop of Mrs. Stewart's goes a long way. When your vision isn't as good as it used to be, it's easy to add a little bit too much. Which she did. She wound up looking like Marge Simpson with nice blue hair. I tried to wash it out but it just had to wear off. I was relieved to see that when her hair dried, the blue wasn't quite as blue. But it was still eye-catching. And not in the way she would've wanted. I hoped she didn't turn out to be a bad example for some kid.

"Life is like a camera. Just focus on what is important. Capture the good times. Develop from the negative and if things don't turn out just take another shot."

~ Author Unknown

CHAPTER 8

"Stand up straight."

My posture as a child was bad and I can't say it has improved much with age. But Mom never gave up on me. When telling me to stand up straight didn't work, she tried other methods. She would take me by the shoulders, push my shoulders back against a wall and make me practice having good posture. She would make me walk with a book on my head. I think I was the only kid who could walk with a book on her head with slumped shoulders. She would tell me to keep my hands out of my pockets, since that made my posture worse. She banned pockets on my clothes since I couldn't manage to keep my hands out of my pockets. Since we made our own dresses (part of being poor), eliminating the pockets was easy. Getting me to stand up straight was not. I never thought I would be fussing at her to do the same.

My mother moved from walking unassisted to walking with a cane, and then to walking with a rolling walker in her eighties. Her posture for an elderly lady was pretty darn good until we got to the walker phase.

A walker is designed to provide stability and safety for the person using it. Well, that only works if you are relatively close to the contraption. My mother seemed to be determined to take the long-arm approach to using a walker. In other words, she would stretch out as far away from the walker as possible. It was as if she thought the thing had cooties. I guess in her mind it did. A walker doesn't conjure up positive images. It is associated with someone being old or disabled. She was both, but probably wasn't ready to admit to the "disabled" label.

"Mom," I would say. "You need to stand up straight when you use your walker. You look like you are about an inch from falling over. Your feet need to be up close to the wheels."

"My feet are up by the wheels. I don't want my ankles to hit them" she would reply.

"No chance of that happening the way you are walking. Let me show you how you look." Okay, that was a mistake. I will admit I exaggerated her stance and posture a bit—but just a bit. She gave me a good fussing about being so fussy. That's not the only time she told me I was too fussy. I explained that I was just trying to encourage her to walk more safely. Then I showed her how hard it would be to keep herself from falling if she was positioned too far behind her walker. She knew that a fall would only spell disaster for her.

"Please stand up straight," was all I had to say after that.

"You've done it before and you can do it now. See the positive possibilities. Redirect the substantial energy of your frustration and turn it into positive, effective, unstoppable determination."

~ Ralph Marston

The dogs loved when Mom cooked, helped in the kitchen or sat down with a plate of food. Here is Katie with a sprinkling of cheese on her head.

CHAPTER 9

"Hang up your clothes."

As an adult, I am a very neat person. I like things organized and clean. Clothes are hung up, socks are matched, towels are folded and things are hung in the closet with a focus on organization. If you ask me where the spaghetti is in my pantry, I could tell you the exact location. That is, if I had spaghetti in my pantry. People who know my pantry provisioning skills know that there is no spaghetti there. But that's another story. Suffice it to say I did not inherit my mother's need to have a full pantry, full freezer, and full refrigerator, nor the provisioning skills to do it right.

As a kid, I was a slob. Clothes came off me and dropped onto the floor, the bed, the chair—wherever was convenient to where the disrobing occurred. I didn't pick them up until it was laundry day or until Mom yelled at me to hang up my clothes. I remember stuffing clothes under my bed so my room looked clean with no clothes in sight. Actually, laundry day didn't help too much because the clean clothes somehow never got put away either.

I know exactly what happened to change my slovenly ways. It was my dear friend Luke G. For a while, he and I were roommates in Mobile, Alabama. His grandmother owned some rental houses and she offered us the opportunity to live in one of them in exchange for doing some work on the house. Luke and I were just friends. He had his bedroom and bathroom and I had mine at the opposite end of the house. He was a neat, orderly roommate, and I was a slob. I was shocked the first time he told me I needed to make my bed in the morning.

Luke had well-honed housekeeping skills and he knew how to keep the house looking great. I was used to waiting for everything in the house to look like a disaster area, and then cleaning it up. Luke would have no part of that. If I was going to live in that house, I was going to have to keep things clean and neat. I can never thank Luke enough for pushing me.

I remember returning to Mom's house to visit and often finding it in need of cleaning. I would walk in the front door, give Mom a hug and a kiss, and start cleaning things. The whole time I was cleaning, I would be mentally chewing out whichever sibling had been there last for not cleaning, or for leaving things in such deplorable shape.

One night, I was on the phone with my husband, complaining about the house and all the cleaning I had been doing. He gave me a startling suggestion. "Honey," he said, "did you ever think that maybe your mom is not the neatest person in the world?" At first it made me mad. My husband was disparaging my dear, sweet mother. Then as I had time to ponder what he said, I realized he was right. Mom really wasn't a great housekeeper. It had never been her priority. I got a lot of genes from my mom, and I am sure that's where my slob genes originated. At least I am living proof that you can overcome them.

Back when Mom was able to hang up her clothes and keep her room clean, she didn't. Church clothes would come off, then onto the bed, the chair—wherever was convenient to where the disrobing occurred. Does this sound familiar?

"Mom, hang up your dress when you take it off," I would tell her as we arrived home after church.

"I always do," she would reply. I would make a mental note to go in and hang up her dress later in the afternoon.

I would do her laundry for her and give her the clean laundry to put away. Mom's occupational therapist suggested we use chores like that to keep her moving. She would take her laundry basket into her room and come back for a rest. "I'll put those clothes up later," she would tell me. Much later, I would think to myself, like never. But giving her the benefit of the doubt, I would wait a day or so before I checked on the status of her laundry and her room. It was not unusual to find that she had not only left the clean laundry in the laundry basket, she had also forgotten it was clean and put dirty laundry on top of it. The silver lining was that at least she was making an attempt to get dirty clothes in the basket.

I used to vacation at a working cattle ranch to play cowgirl for a week at a time. The guests contributed their underwhelming cowboy skills to jobs like rounding up cows in the fall, pushing cows out to pasture in the spring, and our favorite, roping and branding the calves. I commented to the ranch owner, Leo H., one day during branding season that it must save him considerable payroll to have the guests help with the cows. He laughed out loud. I didn't get the humor until he explained that having the guests help out made things twice as hard and generally took twice as long. But guests paid him for the privilege to be a temporary cowboy/cowgirl, which funded his small cattle operation. It allowed him to keep doing what he loved.

With Mom, having her help took twice as long, made things at least twice as hard, and I can assure you made more than twice the mess. I remember one day she was making pimento cheese. It required grating cheese, which she did manually with a rotating cheese grater. All the dogs were sitting under the table catching cheese as it dropped. I saw my dog Katie had grated cheese on her head. Here is my Facebook post for that day:

Why does my dog Katie have grated cheese on top of her head?
a) mom's been cooking again…
b) the other dogs haven't noticed Katie has cheese on top of her head…
c) Katie hasn't noticed she has cheese on top of her head…
d) all of the above.

So while it complicated even the simplest tasks to have her help, it allowed me to keep doing what I loved—spending time with the woman who gave me the sloppy genes.

CHAPTER 10

"Don't talk with your mouth full."

sn't it amazing how children can talk and eat at the same time? There must be countless little pouches in a child's mouth wherein food can be temporarily stored in order to utter important tidbits like, "Sandra gave her Brussels sprouts to the dog." Or in my case, "Why do I have to do the dishes again?!" I always hated washing dishes as a child. Matter of fact, I still do.

My parents felt it was important to eat as a family around the family dining room table. It was a big table and we all had our place. The table also served as a place to fold laundry and a place to pin patterns to fabric when working on a new dress. In the event of severe weather, the kids were sent under the big dining room table since it was our tornado/hurricane safety zone. If that table could talk, what tales it could tell.

My parents also felt it was important to try to make fine, upstanding citizens out of the near-savages their children could be. You were expected to eat politely, pass the food when asked, not reach across your sibling's plate, not chew with your mouth open, and not talk with your mouth full. Violations meant you were probably going to have to wash dishes.

It's a curious thing that some elderly people discount or forget the rules they once imposed.

My mother did not like wearing her dentures. This made for lengthy chewing episodes for all but the softest foods. That didn't bother her at all. She was always a slow eater. She was also not bothered at all by holding a conversation while she was eating. Some days I would just stare in disbelief. I also remembered what she told me about being so fussy. But when she got to the point where I really couldn't understand what she was saying, it was time for, "Mom, don't talk with food in your mouth."

I have to admit I was treading on thin ice when I chastised her for talking with her mouth full. But sometimes, thin ice feels good under your feet. Plus, I knew I was going to have to wash the dishes anyway.

Mom with all five children in 1963. Next to Mom on the right is Sarah, the eldest at age 7. The youngest, Lloyd, was just a few months old. Mom came from a large family and wanted to have several children. She was advised against further pregnancies after her fifth child. She was 41 during her last pregnancy.

CHAPTER 11

"Don't burp out loud."

Heathens. That's what my brothers Luther and Lloyd seemed hell-bent on becoming. They had company, though. I was the ultimate tomboy as a kid. Some would argue I never outgrew it.

My brothers and I developed burping skills that would make the drunkest sailor proud. We prided ourselves on being able to convert belches into words and phrases. Of course, this was all done outdoors, or at least outside of Mom's hearing range. Burping aloud was not allowed. Period. Conversing in belches would get us sent to our rooms. Or worse—sent out to pick a switch off one of the switch bushes. Switches hurt!

Even when we emitted a small, half-suppressed, unintentional burp, we were instructed to say, "Excuse me," and that was usually followed by "You were not raised on a farm." We didn't get the connection to farming and burping aloud, but I know my brothers and I thought that farming must be a pretty neat way to live.

I cannot describe my shock the first time I heard my mother let out a loud burp. It ranked right up there with the first time I heard her say "Shit!" I was speechless. Then I decided that she must have accidentally burped, and that the offending gas missile escaped her lips before she had a chance to clamp them down. I was wrong.

Her inclination to burp aloud actually started with small, hissing burps. She would let the burp slide through her lips and whistle through her teeth. Of course, that was back when she wore her teeth. This made a unique sound, but it was not particularly offensive. It sounded like the burp just crept up on her and slid out unexpectedly.

Maybe she graduated to full-blown burps and belches when she quit wearing her teeth. That would certainly change the tenor of a burp. She moved very quickly to burping a lot and burping loudly. I remember telling her, "Mom, do you remember what you would say to us if we burped out loud?"

"What?" she would reply. Actually, "Huh?" would be her first reply; then after I repeated the question, she would say, "What?" Like she didn't remember the scowl and the scorn heaped upon an unsuspecting burping child.

"You taught us to burp with our mouth closed and say excuse me," I would remind her.

"You weren't an old woman" was her response. Well, I couldn't argue with that. Then she developed the worst case of burping I had ever heard. And I've heard some good ones. At first, I kept my mouth shut. But then it actually escalated to a ridiculous level. About that time, she started having problems eating. Nothing sounded good to her, nothing tasted good, and when she did eat, she couldn't eat very much. But she could burp with the best of them.

I knew something was wrong, so I got on the Internet and started searching for answers to these symptoms. Don't you love "Dr. Google?" He lets you self-diagnose with just a few keystrokes. I didn't find anything on the Internet that looked good relative to her symptoms, so I made an appointment for her to see her doctor. She didn't think it was necessary (see "Yes, you have to go to the doctor"). The doctor ordered some tests and very shortly thereafter called to tell me to get Mom into her office ASAP.

Waiting for an appointment when you know the news must be bad is unsettling. Fortunately, we were able to get in the next day. It turned out that Mom had severe issues with her gallbladder, and had a very large hiatal hernia. So we were headed to the hospital, surgery, and hopefully a return to normal eating habits. I was also hoping that this would cure the big old burps she was belting out. But that was not to be. In the privacy of her home, Mom still burped like those heathen Bullock boys did when we were kids. But after all, she was raised on a farm.

My dad loved his boys! This picture was taken in 1963 and shows what a proud papa he was. He would eventually teach the boys all sorts of manly skills, including how to be gentlemen.

Going to church was very important to my mother. She loved her faith and she lived her faith. She always sat in the second row and could sing most hymns by memory. She was a founding member at Palm Chapel Primitive Baptist Church in Crestview, FL. When her health prevented her from attending services, the pastor and deacons would bring audio recordings of the services to her. Such acts of kindness meant so much to her.

CHAPTER 12

"You'd lose your head if it wasn't screwed on."

opelessly scatterbrained. I think that phrase succinctly describes most young children. Focus is a learned behavior, and some kids never learn it. Now, I am not talking about ADD or ADHD or any other kind of "D" that kids are diagnosed with these days. I am talking about focusing as a general life skill used to prevent such disasters as losing your church shoes, your report card, your homework assignment, or your Brownie uniform.

Kids lose things that are needed RIGHT NOW.

"Sandra, where are your church shoes?" Mom would yell as she was ushering the brood of kids out to the station wagon.

"Maybe they are in the car?" I would respond hopefully. "I had them last Sunday." Secretly I was hoping that if we got in the car and the shoes weren't there we could just skip the formality of shoes for that day.

"They are not in the car. You would lose your head if it wasn't screwed on!"

Mom was right. I wasn't particular about where I left my stuff at that point in my life. And since we had a small house, there weren't too many places where stuff could hide. In my case, a lot of stuff wound up under the bed. It seemed like a good place at the time.

My mother needed assistance dressing starting in her late eighties. She was fairly capable of putting clothes on and taking them off. What happened before putting them on and after taking them off was my department.

When we were getting Mom dressed to leave the house, it was best if I picked out her clothes (see "Are you going to wear that?"). In addition to clothes, I had to locate her dentures and her shoes.

She hated wearing her dentures so she would remove them as soon as she could. This might be in the car, in the bathroom, in her bedroom, or while she was walking from one place to another. In other words, she was not particular about where she left them. Her priority was always getting them out of her mouth.

For a while, I thought her aversion to dentures was due to them not fitting well. I made appointments for adjustments, and eventually we had a new set of dentures made by a highly regarded prosthodontist. It made no difference. In fact, I think she disliked the new dentures even more.

One of the lessons I learned from caring for my mother was to take care of my teeth. Her dentist had a great piece of advice on caring for teeth. He said, "You should only take care of the teeth you want to keep." Well, I want to keep all of mine.

I had a routine for getting Mom ready for church on Sunday. I found that being routine-oriented helped me get things done without forgetting something.

Our weekend routine started with a bath on Saturday. We didn't need any last-minute bathing on Sunday morning. I woke her up early on Sunday so she didn't have to rush. We had a leisurely breakfast and watched The Weather Channel. I picked out her clothes, got her a new pair of stockings, and checked her hairdo. Mom had one of those "little old lady" hairdos that tended to get pushed up in the back when resting her head on the recliner. Think of an erected crest on a cockatiel and you'll have the picture.

My last thing in our Sunday morning prep was asking her if she had her dentures. "I think so," she would respond.

"'I think so' is not a yes. We can't leave until we find your dentures." If we were late for church, I knew it would be my fault somehow.

"Maybe they are in my purse. I had them last Sunday. Did you look in the bathroom?"

"Mom, I haven't looked for them at all. Where did you have them last?"

"Well, did you look by my chair?"

"Mom, you would lose your head if it wasn't screwed on."

"Some days I think I might lose my head anyway," she would say. She was right. Something was always in need of being found— dentures, shoes, ID card, favorite CD. Fortunately, she had a small house and there weren't too many places to look.

So we would go through the frenzy of searching all known "drop points" for her dentures. I always wondered if she was not secretly hoping they would remain at large and she could forego the formality of dentures for that day.

Luckily, a trip I took to Hawaii helped solve that weekly dilemma. While in Hawaii, I found Mom a very pretty quilted, zippered case that was the perfect size for her dentures. The case stayed in her purse unless it was being washed. She popped her dentures out as soon as we got to the car. Instead of wrapping them in a handkerchief or sticking them in a pocket of her purse, she would put them in the case. It was one less thing I had to find on Sunday morning.

CHAPTER 13

"You have had enough sugar today."

W hat kid doesn't love sweets? I know my sweet tooth was the first one to sprout. My mother was a great cook but she didn't make a lot of sweets for us. I think when you have five kids, none of them needs sugar to add to the excitement.

The church we attended as children had a potluck lunch after services on Sunday. There was a long dining room table where all the food was laid out buffet style. At the far end of the table were all the desserts. While the food was being set out, the kids hung out at the dessert end of the table. Mom was generally preoccupied with setting out her basketful of food so we were free to fill our plates with whatever we wanted. And we wanted sweets. I still love the sight of a chocolate cake on the lunch table.

We were even brave enough to head back to the dessert end of the table for seconds. Not that we didn't eat other things. We usually made room for a piece of fried chicken or a slice of meatloaf. But we were always on a mission for sweets. By this time, though, Mom was aware of our activities and would cut us off. "You have had enough sugar today," she would tell us.

Usually when one of us was being chastised about eating too much sugar, the others took advantage of Mom's temporary distraction and grabbed one more cookie. Contraband sweets are always the sweetest.

I don't think Mom had a sweet tooth until she developed borderline diabetes. Isn't that the way things go?

She went through some severe gastrointestinal issues that left her with no appetite. We searched for anything she would eat. We were even willing to include a sugary snack if that meant getting some calories into her. We found a brand of rice pudding that she really liked. It came in small pre-packaged containers so she couldn't eat much at a time. And if she ate one cup every day or two, it didn't cause problems.

My mother quit eating at the dining room table when my dad died in the early 1980s. She said it was too lonely at the table and she just preferred to eat in her recliner. That was when she was able to live by herself. By the time she needed a caregiver, she was firmly entrenched in her "nest." That's what we called the area around her recliner. As her mobility declined, she kept more and more stuff around her chair. It literally looked like a cluttered nest at times.

So for the last few years, someone typically brought Mom's food to her while she was in her recliner. This was another safeguard against her eating too much sugar.

But apparently, the rice pudding sat in the refrigerator and called her name.

"Sandra," she would call out to me. "Bring me some of that rice pudding."

We were thrilled when her appetite was good, so I was happy to get her a container of rice pudding. Then I started noticing Mom ambling slowly to the refrigerator a couple of times a day. Then I made a point to notice what she was getting out of the refrigerator. Rice pudding.

I thought it might be just a temporary thing. She tended to get tired of snacks that she ate frequently. Boy, was I wrong.

When I made out our grocery list, I'd ask her what she wanted to eat during the upcoming week.

"Get some of that rice pudding," she would tell me.

"Where's that rice pudding?" was the first thing she would ask when I got back from the grocery store. I knew I had to cut her off. I put the rice pudding in a remote corner of the refrigerator. Her vision was so poor that if it wasn't in view, she typically couldn't find it. She rummaged through the refrigerator anyway. If she couldn't find the rice pudding, she would call out for me.

"Sandra, where is that rice pudding?"

"Mom, you have had enough sugar today. How about some peanut butter crackers?"

"I haven't had anything sweet today!" she would proclaim innocently. Mom never had been one to tell fibs, but this was a case where I wondered if some of her memory lapses were convenient.

"Well, trust me on this one. You have had too much sugar so let's save the rice pudding for tomorrow."

If she were hungry, I would fix her something that wouldn't drive her blood sugar up too much. And I was thankful that she wanted something to eat. But it didn't take long before she would leave her recliner nest and I would see her slowly ambling into the kitchen again. I knew what she was after. After all, contraband sweets are always the sweetest.

Mom during her college years. She worked in the cafeteria during college, where she further honed her baking skills. They were legendary. She managed to keep a trim figure for most of her life but she told me she always struggled with her weight. I inherited that challenge from her as well.

CHAPTER 14

"Tell me a story."

We loved my parents' stories. They both grew up in interesting times and in interesting places. My mother in particular had great stories from growing up in the mountains of north Georgia. In addition to standard children's stories, we got stories such as the time she came across her cousin's moonshine still while they were out hiking. My dad was in the Air Force and had traveled to exotic places. We visited many places and exciting times through my parents' stories.

I remember Mom talking about her college days, telling me she went to college without ever having attended classes beyond the sixth grade. Mom attended elementary school in a one-room schoolhouse. When she was in sixth grade, many of the local men left for the war. Women were called upon to take over jobs vacated by the departing soldiers. The teacher of her one-room schoolhouse left for one of those jobs. There was no one left in their community to teach grades 1-6 at the rural school.

The school superintendent offered the job to my mom. She was the best sixth grade student so he felt she could teach grades 1-6. Mom was excited about the possibility of teaching, but she was certain her father would not permit it. Her father believed that women only needed a little bit of education. Mom would be needed on the farm.

The superintendent visited my grandfather and told him that Mom would be compensated for teaching and would be able to help the family farm by having an income. Grandpa agreed and Mom's teaching career began. By the time the regular teacher returned, Mom was almost old enough to have graduated from high school. The superintendent told her that if she would study and get her high school equivalent, he would get her a college scholarship. Mom went on to obtain her GED, a college scholarship, and a college degree.

So Mom went to college, graduated, and had a long teaching career, all without being formally schooled herself after the age of twelve. I wondered what other stories she had that I didn't know about. I found a book called The Story of a Lifetime, which contains questions about your life. We spent many fun hours working through these questions so I could discover and document the rich stories of her lifetime.

When she reached her nineties, she seemed to have problems holding a conversation. It was as if she couldn't think of anything to talk about. I pulled out The Story of a Lifetime and used its many diverse questions to get Mom talking and keep her engaged. I found out so many things I didn't know about my mom. One day we were on a roll and she was really enjoying answering the questions I posed. So, I decided to ad-lib and put my own question out there.

"Mom," I said. "Were you afraid of having sex for the first time?"

She stopped and thought for a moment, then with a grin said, "I think your daddy and I both were, but we got over it."

Priceless.

I love telling stories and I love a good adventure. Adventures and stories go hand in hand. Mom didn't have to ask me to tell her a story. I usually had a variety of tales from wherever my recent travels had taken me.

The funny thing about telling Mom stories is that she didn't always hear what I say. If she didn't hear me, she usually asked me to repeat myself (see "Don't say 'Huh'."). One night, I was telling her about hiking in bear country and having to carry bear spray. She said to me, "I just don't understand how hairspray can stop a bear."

"Not hairspray, Mom, bear spray," I told her.

"Well, what the heck is bear spray?"

Or the time when she asked me what I was eating. "Cashews," I responded.

"Cherries?"

"No. Cashews."

"I know you didn't say cow pies??"

"NO, MOM. C-A-S-H-E-W-S."

"Oh. Well, you don't have to yell."

We had some funny misinterpretations, whether during sharing stories, cooking ideas, or just general conversation. But that, as Rudyard Kipling said, is another story. And I did have to yell.

Mom (the tallest person, on the far right in this picture) taught grades 1-6 in a one-room schoolhouse in rural Georgia. We think this photo was taken in 1937, when Mom was 15 years old. She started teaching at age 12.

CHAPTER 15

"Are you going to take a bath?"

I am from the generation of kids who grew up playing outside. No one had a computer. We were not allowed to spend hours in front of the television. We played hard and got dirty. And we hated to bathe, mainly because we had to come inside early to bathe.

There was one bathroom in our house for most of my childhood. You did not want to be the first one to take a bath since that meant coming in really early. You also did not want to be the last one because there would be no hot water left. We often tried to scoot around the issue of bathing by saying we would wait until the water heated up again. Mom was onto that scam. "Are you going to take a bath?" was actually an order: "You are going to take a bath." We only had to be told once. Mom had a good memory back then. Or maybe it was a good nose.

Bathing for an elderly person tends to be a dangerous activity. For my mom, who had severe mobility impairment, it was downright treacherous. I think she dreaded the whole routine. I know I did. Every bath was an opportunity for a fall. We had all the right equipment for a safe bath, but that made it only slightly less scary for me.

My mother was from the generation that took a weekly bath, and as a child that was usually in a tub with water heated on the stove. She believed that a weekly bath was all she needed unless there were extenuating circumstances. Such as spreading manure on your garden. I tried to manage two baths a week for her, but it was a battle. She was really good about getting her Sunday-go-to-meeting bath on Saturday. Trying to work another in during the week reminded me of the excuses we made when we were kids.

"It's too cold this morning."

"I'll do it tomorrow morning."

"Why do I need a bath? I took one three days ago."

I learned that Mom didn't want to smell like she hadn't had a bath. So instead of asking her if she would take a bath, I would just say, "You smell like you haven't had a bath." It worked every time and I only had to say it once.

It looks like I didn't care much for baths either. This photo was taken in early 1958. Mom told me she loved everything about being a mother. It shows in her face in so many pictures.

CHAPTER 17

"Are you going to wear that?"

remember a movie called Wild at Heart. It starred Nicolas Cage and Laura Dern. One of the lines from that movie about wearing a snakeskin jacket summarizes my philosophy on the clothes I wore as a child:

"It's a symbol of my individuality and my belief in personal freedom."

I did not have a snakeskin jacket as a child. But I made up for it. My mother taught all the girls to sew. In the early stages of my sewing career, my fabric and pattern choices were closely supervised, as was the length of any skirt or dress. When I reached the level of independence that included buying my own fabrics and patterns, things changed. So did my hemlines.

I was a teenager in the early seventies. My generation loved miniskirts. So did I. If you could sit on the hem of your skirt, it was too long in my opinion. Several years ago, I found one of my dresses from that era. It was actually shorter than some of the shirts in my closet. No wonder I got stopped at the door on many occasions and asked, "Are you going to wear that?" Well, sometimes it was more like, "You are not leaving the house until you put on something decent!"

We had to provide hands-on help for Mom to pick out her clothes. Not because she had bad fashion sense or poor taste, but because she couldn't see well enough to discern colors and patterns. Whether she was picking clothes out to wear or selecting something to purchase, she needed some adult supervision.

Back when she picked out her own clothes to dress for church, there was more than one occasion when she ambled out of her room with the most bizarre combination of colors and patterns.

"I can't find my belt. Would you go look for it?"

"Sure, Mom, but which part of that outfit am I trying to match? Are you really going to wear that?"

"Well, what's wrong with it?" she would ask with a confused tone to her voice.

"I just think we can find you a blouse that matches the skirt a little better. I'll find one when I find your belt." I probably should have looked for her dentures at the same time.

My brother Lloyd, in an outfit worthy of the question, "Are you going to wear that?" This was taken in 1969 when Lloyd was six years old. Fortunately, his fashion sense improved over the years.

CHAPTER 17

"Yes, you have to go to the doctor."

All of the children in my family managed to grow up with relatively few illnesses and injuries. Considering how rambunctious we were, that was a small miracle. We all hated wearing shoes, so injuries to toes and feet were the most common problem.

We didn't have much experience going to the doctor, so when something came up that might involve a trip to the doctor, we were terrified. We also had to go to the hospital on the Air Force base, which meant we would be hanging out in a waiting room for a long time. That meant giving up valuable playtime and possibly getting a shot. We had to be forced to endure a trip to the doctor.

My mother tended to be very stoical about her medical conditions. I guess that's where I got my "grin and bear it" tendencies. The downside was she could get very miserable before she told me that she felt bad or that something might be really wrong.

"I think we need to go see the doctor, Mom." I always tried to start with a suggestion and hope for her to agree with me.

"Maybe we should wait another day," Mom would respond. "I don't think I need to go to the doctor."

"What makes you think you will be better in a day?" She would usually shrug when I asked. She didn't want to be a bother to anyone.

"Mom, you need to go to the doctor. I will call and see when we can get an appointment."

And so it went. I wondered, if she could still drive and do for herself, would she still want to wait another day? With many elderly people, it's hard to figure out why there is a hesitation about going to the doctor. Are they afraid of the news they will get? Are they worried about the expense? Are they still afraid of shots?

Other than routine exams, I had to press the issue to get Mom to see a doctor. However, there was never an instance when the outcome wasn't worth forcing Mom to endure an office visit. It didn't make me happy to be right, either. I'd take a false alarm on health any day over being right.

If you wait to do everything until you're sure it's right, you'll probably never do much of anything."

~ Win Borden

CHAPTER 18

"Do you want me to go in the exam room with you?"

Remember when you finally reached the age when you could go into a doctor's exam room by yourself? Remember walking into the room feeling so grown-up but kind of wishing your mom was with you? What if the doctor asked you something you didn't know? What if you had to take off your clothes? What if you had to get a shot!?

I remember begging my mom to let me get my ears pierced. When she finally agreed, it was under one condition—that I go to the doctor to have it done. No ear-piercing at the mall for me. She didn't want me to get an infection and have an ear fall off.

I was so excited about getting my ears pierced but hated the thought of going to the doctor. Our family doctor was really old. But the desire to have pierced ears won out and I went to the local doctor. I didn't want Mom to go in the exam room with me, but only because I was afraid she would change her mind about piercing. Truth is, I would have loved having her there.

Giving an elderly parent as much independence as possible is treating them with respect. Letting them go into an exam room without you is asking for trouble.

When we had to make a special trip to the doctor, something was wrong. We would have already gone through the "Yes, you have to go to the doctor" conversation. So, almost without fail, we would get to the exam room and the conversation would go something like this:

Doctor: "Hi, Mrs. Bullock, how are you doing?"

Mom: "I am fine."

Me: "No, Mom, you're not fine. You haven't been able to eat for two days."

Doctor: "Are you having any pain?"

Mom: "No."

Me: "Mom, remember you said you haven't slept for the last two nights because of pain?"

Doctor: "When was your last bowel movement?"

Mom: "Yesterday."

Me: "Mom, remember you said you haven't been able to poop since Sunday?"

I think any physician who deals with geriatric patients is accustomed to this kind of conversation. When I first started caring for my mother, I would try to let her go into the exam room by herself for her routine checkups. Afterward, I would ask her about the exam. She never asked the doctor any questions, never told the doctor about anything unusual she was experiencing, never asked what the results of her lab work meant. So I started going in the exam room with her.

I would still let her answer the questions posed by her doctor. I felt a lot better, though, since I was there to correct her answers and add substance to help the doctor understand her total health picture.

Of course, as her health declined, it became absolutely necessary for me or a sibling to accompany her into the exam room. When she was hospitalized, that need shifted into overdrive.

I have a lot of respect for healthcare workers. They have a tough job. Healthcare workers are like employees of any other profession— there are good ones and there are bad ones. There are nurses and nursing assistants who are observant, concerned, and responsive. Then there are those who put in their hours so they can get the hell out of Dodge. I encountered both types, and all types in between, during Mom's hospitalizations.

There was no way I would have left my mother in a hospital by herself. You need to be very aware and self-sufficient to have a successful stay in a hospital. It's great that there is a button with each hospital bed so the patient can summon help. But if you can't see to find the button, or if you are too disoriented to know how to push the button, then what good is the button?

Elderly patients need someone to help them in any healthcare setting. Mom had several stints at skilled nursing facilities following hospital stays. The skilled nursing facility housed elderly patients with varying degrees of conditions, including hospice patients. After spending many hours at the skilled-nursing facility, it became obvious that the patients who seemed to fare better were the patients who had a family member or other caregiver checking on them regularly. It just doesn't matter how good the facility is rated. There will always be staffing issues and more demands on the staff than can be met.

I also decided, after spending so many hours and days at skilled nursing facilities, that everyone should be required to work or volunteer at a nursing home before they reach the age of forty. That will accomplish a couple of things. Firstly, it will make you want to take better care of yourself. You can die young or you can die trying. If you are going to die trying, you will have a better chance of succeeding if you take care of your health. Secondly, it will give you a real picture of what aging looks like. If you have a parent, it will help you understand and prepare for what's to come. Another benefit is that if you are lucky enough to die trying instead of dying young, this will help you prepare for what you might personally experience as an elderly person. When is the last time someone went into an exam room with you? You might want to get used to the idea. Or die trying.

The Bullock kids: from left to right, Sarah, Sandra, Luther, Sharon, and Lloyd in 1963.

CHAPTER 19

"I know you're too old to wear diapers."

don't remember transitioning from diapers to big-girl panties. I have pictures of me as a toddler in big, saggy (and probably soggy) diapers. Based on that, I have to think it was thrilling to move into the realm of real panties. Mom said that once I started wearing panties, one of my favorite things to do was to take my panties off and wear them on my head. She said I told her they were too hot. I wonder what the neighbors thought.

My parents used to tell me wearing panties on my head turned my hair red. At the time, I believed them. Mom endured my strange ways because she knew I was too old to wear diapers. If I'd had a child, I think I might have left my kid in diapers for a while longer.

I guess if we are fortunate to live long enough, we will eventually have a problem with incontinence. No matter how realistic that sounds, I don't think anything prepares you for helping a parent put on a diaper. One lesson that I (and the marketing folks) learned is not to call them diapers. I referred to them as "disposable panties" when I was talking to Mom.

It took a while for her to accept that she needed these on a daily basis. She would wear them when she had to leave the house. "Just in case," as she said. As the numbers of "accidents" at the house grew, so did the need for disposable panties. Since I already brought her clothes to her in the morning to dress, I just started bringing disposable panties each day too. She told me she had plenty of clean panties and didn't need to wear diapers.

This was one of those moments when honesty was the best policy. Sure, we could change panties many times throughout the day, but the floor and furniture didn't fare well. I explained that to her. I wonder if she recalled me wearing wet panties on my head and not putting me back into diapers.

Back when cloth diapers were the only diapers available—I knew how to rock a soggy diaper! 1958 and just learning to walk.

CHAPTER 20

"Is your diaper dirty?"

I graduated from wearing diapers before my memory graduated to being able to recall questions like "Is your diaper dirty?" I have heard this question countless times, though, whether with my nieces and nephews, the children of my friends, and more recently with the grandchildren of my friends.

From a child's perspective, is there a right answer to this question? If you say yes, does that mean you are in trouble for pooping in your pants, or is it okay since at least you didn't poop on the floor or some other similarly unacceptable place? If you say no, does that mean you are in trouble for not going at all? And if the diaper is dirty, then you are going to be laid out and stripped of diaper and dignity. Even when done gently, it's no fun. But moms know that a little kindness goes a long way.

It's not a natural part of adulthood to endure having someone poke into your privacy to ascertain your potty status. It is not natural in any sense to witness your parent develop a need for personal incontinence products, and certainly not natural to have to intervene in their usage.

To respect Mom, I referred to her "diapers" as disposable panties. She was an adult and deserved to be treated as such. Even if she did just pee on the floor. I never admonished Mom for having an accident. I knew that she felt worse about having the accident than I did about having to clean it up. Of all of the caregiver issues I dealt with, this was one of the most emotionally challenging.

It was embarrassing when I was helping Mom with a potty incident and I could barely keep from throwing up. I think she understood. I have a strong stomach but the combination of cleaning up after my mom and being distressed at her needing to be cleaned up after was gut-wrenching.

There were times when she was very sick and it was necessary for her to wear disposable panties 24-7. "Are your panties dirty?" I would ask, knowing that the odds of them still being clean since the last time I checked were slim.

"I don't know." Now there's another gut-wrencher. Being an adult, being laid out and stripped of diaper and dignity. Being too sick to know your own potty status. I have shed many tears over those occasions. Nothing makes it feel okay. But you have to put on your own big-girl panties and deal with it. And make sure you don't make your parent feel worse about the situation.

During one hospital stay, Mom had a bacterial infection that caused wicked diarrhea. It seemed that I would just finish cleaning her up and cleaning myself up, then going down the hall to cry for a while, when she needed cleaning up again. She and I were both getting dehydrated, Mom from diarrhea and me from crying.

I wanted to keep a bright face and upbeat demeanor when I was in the room with Mom. She apologized many times for needing so many changes and cleanings. I guess I could have waited until a hospital worker came in to do this. Sadly, a patient who needs a diaper change is not a priority. After waiting more than fifteen minutes for a nursing assistant to help, I decided that if it was going to be done quickly, it was going to be done by me. And in this case, done over and over and over again. If you recall the reaction of children when they have a dirty diaper, then think how an adult feels. Immediate action is important from a physical and emotional perspective.

"I am so sorry you have to wipe my butt," Mom would whisper to me.

"Mom, how many times did you change my diaper and wipe my butt?" I asked her.

"More than I could count."

"Then consider this as my repayment for all the times you happily wiped my rear end and changed my diapers without throwing up." We both got a chuckle out of that.

Then she surprised me. My sister Sharon showed up later that day with a dozen red roses for me. It was a gift from Mom with a note that said, "Thank you for wiping my butt." Moms know a little kindness goes a long way.

"Too often we underestimate the power of a touch, a smile, a kind word, a listening ear, an honest compliment, or the smallest act of caring, all of which have the potential to turn a life around."

~ Leo Buscaglia

CHAPTER 21

"Do you want to go to the Emergency Room?"

I can recall only one time when Mom asked me if I wanted to go to the ER. I was home from college for the weekend. My dad, who was mayor of our small town, was in south Florida for a mayors' convention. It was freezing outside and the pipes had frozen. My sister Sarah was having a medical crisis with some "female problems." Mom came into my room and woke me.

"Go help your sister get dressed. I need to take her to the emergency room."

I rolled out of bed and went to Sarah's room, which was at the opposite end of the house. Sarah was bent over crying and obviously in a great deal of pain. She was already dressed and didn't need my help. I was beginning to feel a bit light-headed. I decided I better get back in bed. Sarah was right behind me on our way to the front of the house. I didn't know until then that my emotional response to watching someone I love in pain was to pass out.

I made it to the den, where my brother Lloyd was sitting, when my legs quit moving forward and I felt myself falling. Lloyd thought I was clowning around to make Sarah laugh until I hit the floor. Mom came into the room, looked at me and said, "Do I need to take you to the emergency room too?"

"No," I said. "Just get me back in bed and I will be fine." And I was.

Frozen pipes, fainting, and medical emergencies—when it rained, it poured. But Mom handled it all with a levelheaded demeanor. It's a trait that I inherited. Calm is my middle name. Most of the time, anyway.

My mother didn't want to be a bother to anyone. She had a high tolerance for pain and a low tolerance for fuss.

One of the most challenging elements of being a caregiver for an elderly person is knowing, with any degree of certainty, what you should do in various medical situations. Should you wait to see if the pain passes; do you call the doctor; do you call the EMTs; or do you head straight to the emergency room? Couple that uncertainty with dealing with an elderly parent who doesn't want to be an inconvenience and it results in a cloud of anxiety and anguish.

When I knew that something was definitely wrong with my mom, I knew that some sort of action was required. I was smart enough to know when that involved medical care. What challenged me was knowing which medical care? There were instances when I knew immediately what to do. There were times when I called my sister Sarah or my brother Lloyd and asked for help. There were times when I just went straight for 911.

I always tried to be calm and collected when Mom had a medical emergency. Mom never responded "yes" to the question, "Do you want to go to the emergency room?" It took a calm, reasoned conversation with her to get her to change her mind. When all else failed, I asked her to do it for me. I told her that I just didn't know what I should do and asked her what she would do if our roles were reversed.

"I guess we should go," she would say calmly. I wish I could say I recall only one time when I had to ask Mom if she wanted to go to the emergency room. In fact, there were many. Some of them are more memorable than others. All of them were a test of my ability to stay calm.

There is one funny story out of our ER encounters. My mother was visiting with three of her sisters. They were discussing Mom's most recent trip to the emergency room and the wonderful response by the EMTs, thanks to her Life Alert system. In an emergency, all she had to do was push a button and the EMTs were at her house within minutes.

"I can push a button and have six good-looking men in my living room within five minutes," she told my aunts.

I guess there is always a silver lining.

The Mooney sisters were a strong bunch! From left to right — Rebie (Mom), Senie, Lily, Clara, Hazel, Opal and Edna. They were all very tall women. Aunt Opal was well over 6' tall.

CHAPTER 22

"I can't do everything for you."

"Mom, can you braid my hair?"
"Mom, can you hem my dress?"
"Mom, can you read me a story?"
"Mom, can you show me how to catch a lizard?"

Now multiply those types of questions by five children and you will have an idea of the barrage of requests my mom faced on a daily basis. I think she must have had some supernatural skills to be able to work and raise five kids and keep her sanity.

Mom taught us to do things on our own. Sometimes it worked; sometimes it didn't. I guess each of the kids had his or her moments of being needy. I hope there weren't too many of us being needy at the same time. I remember times when Mom would get frustrated and tell us, "I can't do everything for you."

We needed to learn to do so many things, such as dress hemming, reading, and lizard catching. I learned how to braid my hair, but it never turned out like when Mom did it. I continued to ask my mom to braid my hair as an adult. She could French-braid hair so tightly that it was like having an instant face-lift.

No, Mom couldn't do everything for us. I'm glad she didn't try.

I guess I could have done almost everything for my mom. She could sit in her recliner and not move a muscle. When I first started caring for her, that's pretty much what I did. I thought if I did everything for her, perhaps she would have more strength. It took me a while to figure out that all I was doing was diminishing the capabilities she still had.

"I need a snack," she would say. That was her way of saying, "Would you go get me something to eat?"

In the beginning, I jumped up and got her a snack. Then after a while, I realized that she really needed to move throughout the day. So unless she was feeling poorly, my response changed to, "There are plenty of snacks in the kitchen." That would include plenty of sugar-free rice pudding, by the way. I was so thankful when the sugar-free version showed up at the grocery store. When I added, "Why don't you walk a lap around the inside of the house while you are up?" I could detect a bit of a grimace on her face.

I think this strategy to get Mom moving baffled some of my siblings. When my brother Lloyd was home and Mom would say, "I need a snack," he would start to get up and get her something.

"Lloyd, Mom can get her own snacks. She needs the exercise," I would tell him. Lloyd called me a "meanie" more than once since I didn't wait on Mom hand and foot. But I realized doing everything for her left her with no challenges, no exercise, and very little movement. During one of her stays at the rehabilitation center, I noticed a sign that said, "Movement is Medicine." This is so true for the elderly.

I always did things for her when she wasn't capable of doing them for herself. But even though I could have done everything for her, I am glad I didn't.

Mom was a woman of many talents. She was an expert seamstress and had legendary cooking and baking skills. She taught her daughters to sew and to cook. We made our own clothes for many years.

CHAPTER 23

"It's time we start thinking about somewhere else for you to live."

I was the first child to leave home. I still remember that day very clearly. I was moving from Florida to Alabama to start college. I would be living in the dormitory at the University of South Alabama. I didn't need a lot of stuff, so what I needed was in my car. I was so looking forward to being independent. Still, I cried as I drove away. I have a really wide independent streak. Leaving the comfort and security of home for the big unknown was exciting and frightening. I hoped I was prepared for what was ahead.

Mom didn't have to tell me that I needed to find somewhere else to live. I was chomping at the bit to be on my own. I had siblings who moved out and moved back in. Mom graciously took them back in and uttered a prayer of thanks when they moved out again.

These days, there are many parents who cannot get their kids to leave the house. It's easy to start a conversation with a child by saying, "It's time we start thinking about somewhere else for you to live." If he or she doesn't take the bait, maybe it's time to move on to stronger measures. For an adult child, living at home makes it easier to be unemployed and unfettered by financial obligations. Abigail Van Buren, of "Dear Abby" fame, had a great perspective on this. She said, "If you want your children to keep their feet on the ground, put some responsibility on their shoulders."

We had hoped to keep Mom in her house for the rest of her life. There had been times when she temporarily resided at other places, like the skilled-nursing facility or a sibling's house. She always had better overall health and a happier demeanor when she was living in her own home. That is, until something happened, like one of those emergency room visits or a fall.

My sister Sarah, my brother Lloyd, and I were willing to give up a lot of our lives to stay with Mom at her house. My sister Sharon and my brother Luther had less time available to help with caregiving because of their jobs and families. When the availability of my sister Sarah changed due to her own health issues, we had to start looking for other options. Sarah's inability to care for Mom five months out of the year left a huge gap in the caregiver's calendar.

We considered having Mom live at Lloyd's house in Alabama and hiring a caregiver to stay with her during day on weekdays. Lloyd would take care of her at night. There were a few downsides to this option. Finding the right person who would really care for Mom would be a challenge. Even if we found the right person, there was no certainty that he or she would stay for as long as we needed. In addition, Mom often needed help throughout the night. That's not so bad when you don't have to get up and go to a job in the morning. For Lloyd, though, it would have meant severely interrupted sleep followed by a long day at work.

In addition to those considerations, Lloyd would have to bring Mom back and forth each weekend to attend church. She did not travel well. It was important to Mom that she attend services, though. We needed a solution that included her staying close to her church.

We deliberated on hiring a live-in caregiver to stay with her in her house. We needed someone who would be satisfied living in a bedroom in Mom's house, someone who was trustworthy, since he or she would shop for Mom, someone who would actively and proactively care for her, someone who could tolerate her spoiled Chihuahuas, and someone with a basic understanding of healthcare. Even if we did find someone, we could still be left without a caregiver if he or she didn't work out. We needed a solution that included the probability of being a long-term solution.

Given that, our best option was moving Mom into a skilled-nursing/assisted-living facility. I knew it would take a few months to find a place for her and to handle everything associated with the move. My first hurdle was having the conversation with Mom. I dreaded the thought of it. Mom had told us for years that she wasn't opposed to living in a nursing home. That's easy to say when you don't know if you will ever need to live in a nursing home.

I've learned it's best for me to do things I dread sooner rather than later. It saves a lot of angst and anxiety. On this occasion, there was still plenty angst and anxiety to be had.

I brought Mom coffee in bed and sat down next to her. She asked me how I slept and I told her I had barely slept at all. She asked me why. I started crying, which isn't something I do often. I told her I was so worried about who would take care of her when I had to go back to New Mexico.

"Did Sarah tell you that she isn't going to be able to stay with you after I go home?" I asked.

"No," she responded. "Why can't she stay with me?"

"Well, you know Sarah has health issues. When she had the stroke a few years ago, it damaged the part of her brain that deals with stress and anxiety. She is at the point physically and emotionally that she just can't handle being a caregiver." I held my breath and hoped Mom didn't start crying.

"Why didn't she tell me?" Mom asked.

"I guess because it's a hard thing to tell your mom that you can't take care of her. Sarah probably worried every day about having to tell you. The reason I'm telling you is because we have to talk about what will happen when I go home. It's time we start thinking about somewhere else for you to live."

I very carefully explained the options I had considered and the challenges each one represented. I told her that it seemed the best option was for her to move into an assisted-living facility.

"Why can't I stay here?" she asked.

"Who would stay with you?" I responded.

"I don't need anyone to stay with me."

That wasn't the response I expected. I thought she had a good awareness of the reasons someone was with her all the time.

"Mom, do you remember putting a pot on the stove, then sitting in your chair and falling asleep? Remember the food in the pot burned but I got back here before it started a fire?"

"No, I don't remember that."

"Do you remember all the times you've called one of us in the middle of the night, sometimes multiple times, because you needed something that you couldn't do yourself?"

"I don't need help that often."

"Do you remember taking too much medicine because you forgot you had already taken your medicine?"

"I don't think I've ever done that."

"Why do you think we have taken all of your medicine and manage it for you? You can't see to take medicine correctly, and you can't remember if you've taken it or not. Maybe you don't remember these things, but these are just examples of why you need help. It's why one of us always stays with you now. But since Sarah can't stay anymore and I can't stay here year-round, we need to find a place that you will like and that will help you."

"What about my dogs?"

Mom and I share a love for dogs. I knew this was going to be an issue.

"Mom, we will make sure your dogs are well-loved." I didn't know how, but I could figure that out later.

"Well, if I can't live in my home, I guess I could live in a place that would help me. It will be a lot different, though."

"I am hoping we can find a place where different isn't all that bad."

Mom told me, "Well, I have always been able to deal with whatever was put in front of me. I guess I will be all right."

I knew moving Mom to an assisted-living facility was the best option we had. Still, I cried a lot over this decision. I tried to keep my tears hidden, like crying when I took a shower. I remember going to the gym shortly after having that conversation with Mom. I was on the treadmill at the gym and just started crying. Trying to hide your tears in the middle of a packed gym isn't easy. It gave a new meaning to the phrase, "No pain, no gain."

Leaving the comfort and security of your home for the big unknown can be exciting and frightening. I hoped we were both prepared for what was ahead.

We looked at a few different assisted-living facilities. One of my major concerns was that Mom would not ask for help when she needed it. We knew she couldn't cook for herself or manage her medications. Her short-term memory was basically gone at that point.

One of the nurses at her doctor's office told me of a memory-care facility in our community that had a very good reputation. After checking it out with multiple personal visits, I found that it was exactly the type of place Mom needed. The fact that Mom couldn't remember what she needed was compensated for by staff members who were accustomed to caring for residents with memory issues.

Mom lived there for a few years until a broken leg created health problems that necessitated skilled nursing care in a nursing home. We were thankful for having found a place that cared for her and strived to address her needs and our concerns. They weren't perfect, but I don't think there is a facility that can get everything right and live up to children's expectations for their parent's care. But the staff was genuinely fond of my mother. Any concern we had was easy to bring up to the staff. It wasn't as good as being cared for at home but as an alternative, it worked out well.

"Allow yourself a moment of grief when life's misfortunes visit you. However, do not spend your days building a monument to them."

~Dodinsky

CHAPTER 24

"Don't cry—it will be all right."

The Bullock children were not crybabies. Crying for effect did not buy us time, forgiveness, attention, or sympathy. Crying after you broke something that you'd been told to not touch didn't save you from the punishment for disobeying, even if you did cut your finger. In fact, Mom often told us, "You quit that crying or I will give you something to cry about."

How Mom knew the difference between tears that didn't warrant attention and those that did is a mystery of motherhood I never solved. She had a sixth sense about such things. Perhaps many years as a first-grade schoolteacher helped her hone that sense as well.

Mom always knew that tears associated with emotional angst needed special care. I don't remember crying a lot, but I did have some memorable rivers of tears that Mom helped to soothe. My first big hurt due to a lost love left me bereft at a level I considered beyond solace. Funnily enough, I never dated the boy who broke my heart so badly. He was my friend and I wanted more. When I heard he was dating another girl, I cried for days. Mom told me that I would meet a nice boy when the time was right and that crying was not the answer. I never asked her what the answer was. There was just something in her voice that assured me life would go on, with or without the boyfriend of my dreams. She assured me everything would be all right if I would put myself to "good use." I'm sure it involved washing dishes.

Forty years later, that boy is still one of my friends. He was never my boyfriend. And everything did work out to be all right.

I rarely witnessed my mother cry when I was a child. She was strong emotionally and had such a calm and peaceful way of handling crises. When she cried, we knew that something serious was afoot—a relative had passed or a child was in serious trouble. There were perhaps five times I saw her cry.

When Mom reached her late eighties, she started crying frequently. Sometimes she cried if she was having a lot of pain. Often she cried for what appeared to be no reason at all.

At the assisted living facility, I would arrive to spend the day with her and the staff would tell me that she had been crying most of the morning.

"Mom, what's wrong?" I would ask.

"I'm just sad" she would reply. Or, "I don't know."

By this time, her short-term memory had declined to the point that she couldn't remember if she had had a visitor that day. She would tell me she was lonely and no one came to visit her. This would be during a time when I was spending every day with her. A typical week saw at least two of my siblings visiting from out of town as well.

It was so distressing to me that she thought no one was visiting her. It was emotionally challenging to see her cry about anything.

"Don't cry, Mom. Everything will be all right." I would tell her. "Plus, if you keep crying I'm going to cry too, then we will both be a mess."

"Well, we can't have that," she would reply.

One of my best responses to finding my mother crying was to engage her in an activity to get her mind on something else. If the weather was bad, I would bring fresh green beans and have her help snap them. When the weather was pretty, I took her outside.

Turkey Creek Nature Trail was a nature walk in a big cypress grove close to the assisted living facility. It had an elevated boardwalk that was wheelchair-friendly. Mom loved going to Turkey Creek and being wheeled along the boardwalk through the cypress grove by the river.

There were always children out for a walk (or roll). There were birds that she could not see but could hear. There were squirrels begging for food. I often packed a little snack and we sat by the creek and just enjoyed being outdoors. There were no tears there.

When she cried because of physical pain, that was a lot harder. She had prescription drugs to help ease her pain, but some days that wasn't enough. Her arthritis always flared up when a rainy weather front moved through. She told us her joints could predict the weather.

I can only imagine what's it is like for a mother to watch her child in pain and be unable to alleviate that pain. For me to watch my mother in that situation resulted in my prayers asking for one thing: "God, please take her pain away."

How do you know if God answers your prayers? Sometimes, it's a tangible thing, like Mom having a day when she felt good and had no obvious pain issues. Sometimes, you just have to have faith that a loving God would not let a devout servant such as my mom suffer so much. And some days, your faith is tested.

When Mom cried, sometimes I just held her hands and told her I loved her and everything would be all right. I looked at her and wondered what was going on in her beautiful mind and if my "whole" mom was still in there, or if those parts of her were gone forever. It didn't matter, though. I was going to love her forever and try to make everything all right.

Bedtime hugs for everyone. We always felt loved. Circa 1959.

CHAPTER 25

"I love you."

Those are three little words that mean so much. They can also be three little words that are used with very little substance to back them up—like on soap operas when the tanned, good-looking main character says those words to some gorgeous lady who is about to become Mrs. Main Character #5.

When I look back on my childhood, I don't remember hearing those words very often. What I remember is feeling loved. The way my parents treated each other was the ultimate display of love. I never heard them fight, disagree, or even have cross words with each other. I didn't know how special that was until I became an adult and heard stories from friends about their parents. My parents only raised their voices at us if we were in severe trouble. To this day, yelling is totally foreign to me. Even talking in a loud voice so Mom could hear me felt wrong and disrespectful.

My mother had a way of comforting us that was so loving. She sometimes didn't know what to say but she always knew what to do. It often involved a hug. Her mother was the same way. I still remember how loved I felt when I was embraced by Grandma Mooney or Grandma Bullock. One of the saddest times I remember as a child was being told I was too big to be in my Grandma Mooney's lap. It was such a loving place.

So even though we didn't say "I love you" that much when I was growing up, I got the message. I guess that's one reason being a caregiver to my mom was something I wanted to do. Someone who has so much love and compassion for others deserves the same.

CHAPTER 26

The Final Trade

I don't remember entering this life on earth. Mom told me that I tried to be a breech birth but the doctors managed to get me turned around. I know the first loving hands that held me were Mom's.

The last loving hands Mom held were her children's. Sarah and I held her hands constantly for the last twenty-four hours of her life. When the rest of the family came to be with us in her final hours, we all took turns holding her hands. I remember thinking that she had had a full life, that she was weary, and that her physical condition was torturous to her. It was time to let her go. Sometimes things make sense in your head, but not in your heart. I did not want to let her go, but I did not want her to suffer any more either.

When we knew Mom was dying and had just a few days left on this earth, I could not bring myself to tell Mom she was dying. In the few times when we talked about death, she would say she wasn't ready to go. She had survived so many brushes with death, she may not have realized this situation was different. Should I have told her that her passing was imminent? I've pondered that with tears in my eyes many times. And I always come to the same conclusion—our actions spoke louder than our words, and our actions told her how much we loved her, regardless of when she would die.

We knew her 92-year-old heart was failing. 92 sounds like a long life unless it's your mother's life and the end is near. We spent her last days sitting with her, telling stories and telling her we loved her. Her preacher visited often and brought church members in to sing hymns with her. She told us about hearing her first sermon and crying tears of joy because she knew she loved God. She told of being baptized in the river and even remembered seeing the stones in the clear water. I knew she was not afraid of dying because she believed that a better life awaited her with God. Still, I couldn't tell her that her end was near.

In the last hours of her life, her breathing became very rapid and shallow. She opened her eyes occasionally, but briefly. We all talked, sang and prayed. We wanted her to know we were there with her. When she took what seemed to be her last, shuddering breath and then stopped breathing, we knew she had passed. Tears and wailing filled the room immediately. Then she started breathing again. I think it was her way of saying, "That was a test run. Now pull yourselves together. It's okay." After a few more breaths, she stopped breathing again and we knew we had lost her. I notified the nurse who came into her room and made it official.

I cannot describe how hard it is to hold the hand of a loved one as he or she is dying. I can describe the love that flows when you do. I was overwhelmed with an emotional strength I did not know I possessed. Though Mom was no longer able to communicate in her last hours, I felt such love between us when I held her hand. I wanted her to know we were there with her as she was leaving this world, just as she was with us as we entered this world.

Her family surrounded her as she took her last breaths. Her family surrounded her in the years before that. It did not take her death for us to know the value of her life. We knew its worth throughout our lives as we witnessed the example she set for others.

I did not cry when my mother passed away. For years, the mere thought of losing her brought me to tears. But watching her struggle in her last hours brought me peace when she left us. I did not cry at her funeral. I had attended funerals where I saw a child or a spouse of the departed with dry eyes. That was beyond comprehension, until I experienced my mother's passing. I was so relieved for her to be out of pain, to no longer be struggling, to be moving on to the afterlife she cherished so faithfully. Mom's funeral was held on my father's birthday. We could only imagine their happy reunion in Heaven.

When I think back over the last ten years of caring for my mother, maybe there are things that my siblings and I should have done differently. But what comforts me is knowing we did the best we could. We made decisions with her best interests in mind. There are rarely right and wrong answers to the questions you have when caring for an elderly parent. You have to make a decision and move on. Often when dealing with medical decisions, I would ask the doctor, "If this was your mother, what would you do?" There was never a hesitation when the doctor responded. There is comfort in knowing what someone else would do in any given situation.

If you are caring for an elderly parent, you struggle with decisions. At the end of the day, if you remember the Golden Rule—"Do unto others…"—then your path will become clearer. Not easier, but clearer. I wish you the best.

"My mom is a never-ending song in my heart of comfort, happiness and being. I may sometimes forget the words but I always remember the tune."

~ Terri Guillemets

CHAPTER 27

Lessons learned

Here are some things we learned along the way about caring for an aging parent. These lessons can come in handy in other aspects of your life as well.

1. Some days any calorie is a good calorie.

We worried a lot about getting quality calories into Mom's diet. There were days when we could get only a few bites of anything in her. We tried to limit her sugar intake but other than that, we became willing to sacrifice quality for quantity. Never stop trying to get quality calories consumed and never stop trying to find something—anything—your parent is willing to eat.

2. Pick your battles.

Elderly parents really can be like little kids. I learned to prioritize the issues that were the most important with Mom. Sometimes that was a daily task. If I could get her to eat, then I wouldn't press her to change from her robe to a dress. If I could get her bathed, then I wouldn't press her about eating all her dinner. I learned that getting it all done wasn't as important as I once thought.

3. Be a squeaky wheel (a nice one).

Whether your parent is at an assisted-living facility, a hospital, or a skilled-nursing facility/nursing home, your presence makes a difference. When the staff knows you are going to be there and be involved in your parent's care, they seem more likely to pay attention to your parent. I learned the name of anyone involved in my mother's care and called staff members by name. I think there is an appreciation from staff members for family members who take the time to learn their names. Also, if something does go wrong, knowing the names of those involved is helpful.

4. Ask questions.

If you think something is wrong or "off", ask questions. Why, what, when, where, how—it can make a difference in your parent's health and/or healthcare. When your parent lives in a facility, you have the right to ask questions about your parent's care. If you don't understand something, see something change that you were not aware of, etc., ask. If you want something special done—for example, getting a more compatible roommate—ask.

5. Be involved.

This is particularly important when your parent lives in a facility. These facilities have various activities that can involve family members. Your involvement keeps your loved one on their radar screen.

6. Listen.

We learned so many things about my mother throughout the time we cared for her. She rarely would mention something she actually wanted to do, so when she did, we found a way to make it happen. One of the most surprising things she mentioned was the desire to ride a train. We would have never guessed that! She was still able to travel at that point, so we took a road trip to North Carolina for a ride on a historic steam train. She was like a kid. While you may not be able to do things your parent wants to do, listen for the ones you can make happen.

7. Stay Busy.

There is a lot of downtime when caring for an elderly person. There are flurries of activity, followed by hours of them sleeping or watching TV (or both). As a very active person, this was one of the hardest elements of caring for my mother. I'm not good at sitting still. I found that if I wasn't busy, I tended to think about food. Then I tended to eat said food.

I started working in the yard, cooking meals from scratch, organizing cabinets, closets, refinishing furniture, making quilts, reading, etc. I always had a project in the works. Keeping my mind and hands busy helped keep me sane and helped me avoid weight gain.

8. Familiar things mean a lot.

We found that having some of Mom's favorite pictures, her favorite quilt, favorite snacks, etc., made her transition to facility living much easier. My sister got her a stuffed animal puppy that was her constant companion. She said it was the best-behaved dog she ever had.

9. There is no equal sharing of duties among siblings.

There are five children in our family. Three of us were primary caregivers to our mother. You cannot find peace within the realm of caregiving if you are trying to make the job equal among the caregivers. You all have different strengths, abilities, availability, etc. Find peace with a routine that works for you and remember that you are doing it for love. And forget about resenting siblings who don't help, or don't help enough—you will waste your emotional energy. Ask for their help, but if they can't or won't help, don't dwell on it.

10. Think creatively about challenges and problems.

Remember the old saying, "There's more than one way to skin a cat."? You will find as your parent ages that he/she can't do things as he/she once did. Whether it's mobility, eating, bathing, etc., you will have to find ways to work around obstacles to their daily activities. You can also find ways to enable your parent to participate in activities he/she likes. Mom loved to read. As her eyesight deteriorated, we changed to large print books, and then to audio books. This is an area where having a group of friends and/or family members who can help you with ideas can come in handy. Don't look at the problem as a problem, take it on as a challenge and find a creative solution.

11. Have one person control the finances.

It is important to manage your parent's finances with an eye on long-term needs. The cost of care in any facility is staggering. Whoever manages the money needs to understand how much is needed for current care, and what the options may be when the money runs out. Qualifying for Medicaid takes time and the application process is monumental. It will take careful planning to coordinate your parent's needs and synchronize those needs with available funds. If it's not possible for one person to control the finances, a collaborative approach will work if everyone involved is dedicated to making financial decisions in the best interest of the parent.

12. Look for programs that can help you.

There are so many programs available for the elderly and/or disabled individuals: Meals on Wheels, transportation programs, volunteers who will come read to the elderly, etc. Most areas have a Council on Aging or a similar organization that can help you find services. We also used an adult day care center that Mom really enjoyed. It was a tremendous relief knowing we could run errands for a few hours and be certain Mom was being looked after. Plus, the adult day care center had activities that she truly enjoyed.

From a financial perspective, research any special programs like the Veteran's Benefits Administration Aid and Attendance program. My father was a veteran who retired from the United States Air Force. His service yielded many benefits such as health insurance for my mother, and survivor benefits through his pension.

The fact that I had never heard of The Veteran's Benefit Administration program amazed me. I thought that any benefit for which a veteran or his/her surviving spouse was eligible would have been presented in some way to the eligible party. Not so. I found out about this program on Judge Judy!

So here was a program that would pay an additional pension due to my father's service in the Air Force that we knew nothing about. I had to write Judge Judy a thank-you letter for that tidbit showing up on one episode. I bet she doesn't get many of those.

13. Take a good look—this may be you one day.

While caring for Mom, I often thought about how my life as an elderly woman will be. I am not good at asking for help. I got that from my mom. What could I learn from caring for her that will make it easier for someone to care for me? And what healthy changes can I make to avoid some of the health issues she had?

14. Remember that your elderly parent used to be young.

I think it is too easy to look at elderly people and forget that they were once young and vital and full of hopes and dreams. They are living encyclopedias. Our culture tends to be obsessed with youth, but the real treasures are our elders.

15. Have no regrets.

Some decisions can be changed, some cannot. Hindsight really is 20/20. If you find you should have made a different decision but there is nothing you can do to change what you decided, let it go. If there is a lesson you can learn from your decision-making process, learn it. Don't beat yourself up over what might have been if you had decided differently.

16. Be thankful.

No matter what your caregiving story is, you will grow as a person by caring for another.

17. Enjoy your life after your loved one passes.

For many months after my mother's death, I felt guilty when realizing that I did not have to work my plans around the care of my mother. For years, any trip I planned had to be coordinated with her caregiving. There were times when I was scheduled to get on a plane in a day or two, but she had a health issue that might potentially (and occasionally did) derail those plans. Mom never made us feel guilty. It's okay to feel a sense of freedom when your caregiving days are over. You paid your dues with love.

"Never regret. If it's good, it's wonderful. If it's bad, it's experience."

~ Victoria Holt

PHOTO GALLERY

My mother, Rebie Mooney Bullock and father, Curtis F. Bullock, Jr.
We were fortunate to be raised by such a loving couple. Circa 1953

This picture was taken early in Mom and Dad's courtship.
They had been pen pals for six months before they met in
person. Mom said Dad pulled up to the college in a taxi with
a big red Teddy Bear. "It was love at first sight."

Mom and Dad with their first grandchild Katrina in 1980.
Dad died at age 56 before their grandchildren Jessica,
Holly, Ashley, and Curtis were born.

"School marm" days.

This is one of Mom's annual school pictures. She was a first grade teacher at Shalimar Elementary School for many years.

Mom with her mother, Ollie Weaver Mooney (Grandma Mooney).

Mom and Grandma Mooney years later. It would be
hard to say who made the best biscuits.

The three sisters in 1963; from left to right, Sharon at age two, Sandra at age five, and Sarah at age seven. You can tell from this picture our personalities were very different and still are.

Mom and Dad on their wedding day in 1952. My grandfather, Elder Tandy C. Mooney, officiated. Dad wrote Grandpa Mooney to ask for Mom's hand in marriage. In the letter, he detailed his virtues as a potential husband, but also admitted having tasted whiskey once. "I didn't like it," he noted in the letter. I don't think that as a former moonshiner, Grandpa Mooney would've minded.

Sam the stuffed dog was Mom's constant companion for the last two years of her life. She said he was the best-behaved dog she'd ever had. He was a gift from my sister Sarah. I thought it was a silly gift at the time. I was wrong.

Sam the dog was by Mom's side even in her last days. It was amazing how much comfort this stuffed animal gave her.

Mom with some of her Christmas goodies during our last Christmas together in 2014. The staff members at Westwood Healthcare each adopted a resident and brought him/her a gift. Mom also had gifts from one of the Squadrons at Eglin Air Force Base. She was amazed that people who didn't know her would do such nice things.

My brother Lloyd had asked to use his sick leave on one occasion to stay with Mom. His employer told him his mother was not "immediate family." Since Lloyd was not married and had no children, Mom was his immediate family. He and Mom put together this humorous protest picture. Hopefully, the future will bring changes to presently existing policies which don't define a mother as "immediate family."

My mother loved being a mother, a grandmother, and a great-grandmother. Here she is pictured with her great-grandson Landon and her dog Taffy in 2012. My sister Sharon adopted Taffy when Mom moved into the assisted-living facility. Sharon brought Taffy to visit Mom frequently. Taffy died a few days after Mom died. Tonka, Mom's other dog, was adopted by her veterinarian's assistant.

This
is the kitchen of
REBIE BULLOCK
I Am The Boss!
if you don't believe it...
Start
Something!

My dad had this plaque made for Mom in the 1960's. There was no doubt who was running the show in her kitchen. When she passed away, this plaque moved to my house.

"Grief never ends...but it changes. It's a passage, not a place to stay. Grief is not a sign of weakness, nor a lack of faith...it is the price of love."

~ Darcie Sims

ABOUT THE AUTHOR:

S andra Bullock Smith is a retired human resources executive who currently lives in Santa Fe, New Mexico, with her husband, Mike, and their mongrel pups. A world traveler, angler, adventure junkie, and storyteller, she also works as a crew chief for several endurance running and cycling athletes.

One of her greatest challenges in life was the ten-year period during which she and her siblings cared for their aging mother. This experience led her to pen her first book, *Trading Places: Becoming My Mother's Mother.* She hopes it offers insight and encouragement to anyone involved in a similar labor of love.

She loves to hear from her readers and can be reached at sandrabullocksmith@yahoo.com, or via the book's Facebook page at Trading Places: Becoming My Mother's Mother.

NOTE TO THE READER

Thank you for reading *Trading Places: Becoming My Mother's Mother.* I am grateful for your interest and the time you invested in reading it.

Review it: Now, please go to www.Amazon.com and leave a brief review for the book. Potential readers rely heavily on book reviews when deciding whether they will purchase the book.

Follow it: Visit the book's Facebook page and follow me on Twitter @sbsmithauthor.

Connect with me: Visit my webpage at www.sandrabullocksmith.com

Contact me: I welcome your comments regarding Trading Places. Email me at sandrabullocksmith@yahoo.com

thanks!